SLIDE SHOW

ALL NEWD!

STUDIO NUDES BY Harrison Marks

KODAK

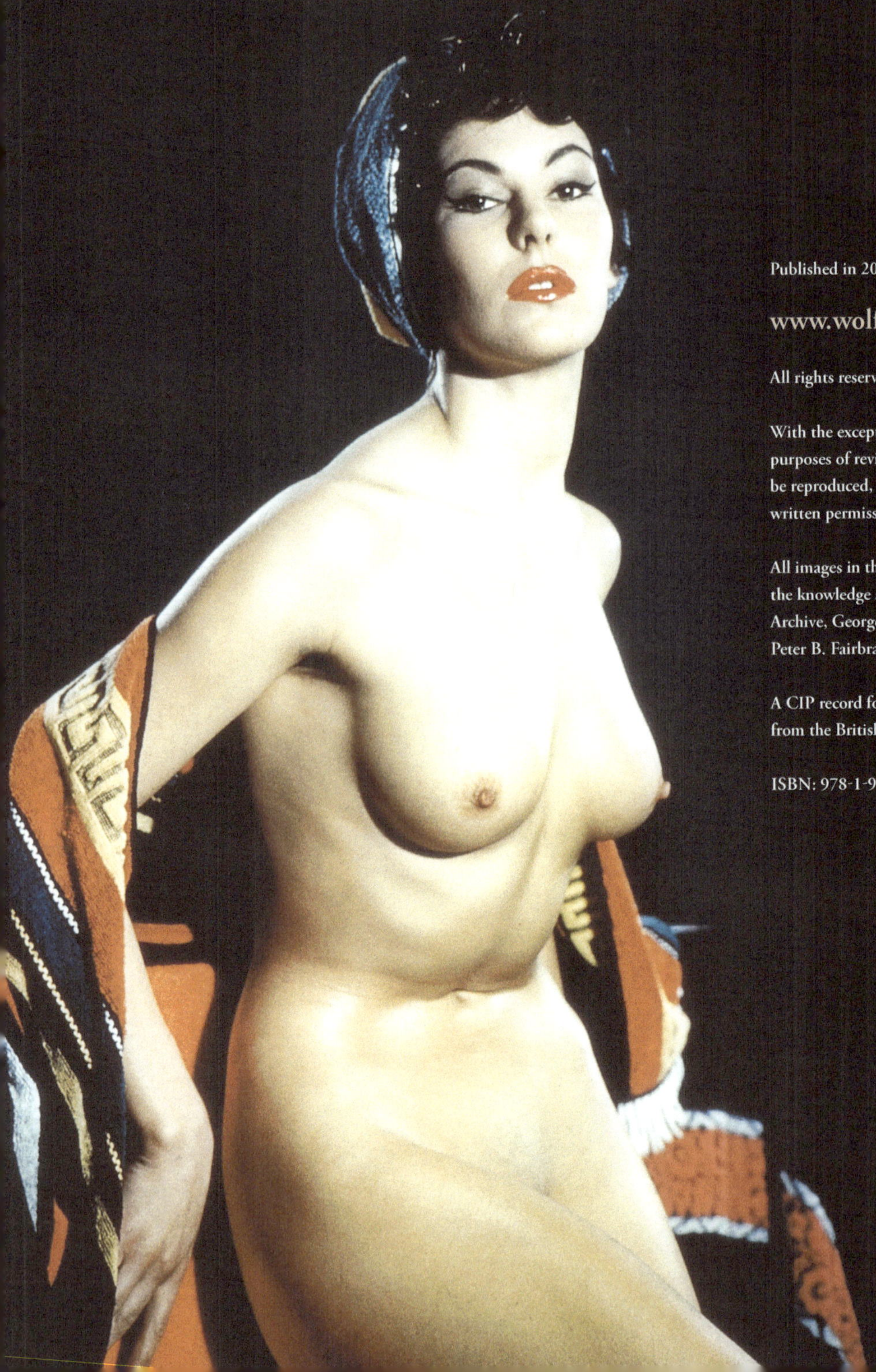

Published in 2021 by Wolfbait Books

www.wolfbait.co.uk

All images in this book have been reproduced with the knowledge and prior consent of the Pamela Green Archive, George Harrison Marks Enterprises Ltd and Peter B. Fairbrass.

A CIP record for this book is available from the British Library.

ISBN: 978-1-9162151-5-3

SLIDE SHOW

ALL NEWD!

STUDIO NUDES BY Harrison Marks

by Yahya El-Droubie

with a foreword by Jean Spaul

WOLFBAIT

UNDER THE COUNTER CULTURE

"PAMAR" COLOUR SLIDES

Photographed

by

Harrison Marks

Foreword

EARLY in my career, I did some modelling, including bikini shots for *Spick and Span*. Looking for more work, I came across George Harrison Marks's studio in Gerrard Street, who promptly booked me for a photoshoot. Most of his work was nudes, and it wasn't long before I was persuaded to go topless and eventually nude.

When George and Pam found out I could type, I ended up working for them in the office. It was around this time that the first few issues of *Kamera* were being produced. Everyone was really excited about it.

I appeared in the early issues and featured on the covers of issues 2 and 27. Around this time, Pamela and George formed Pamar Colour Slides Ltd. The name was arrived at by combining their two names Pam and Marks. It was to handle sales of colour transparencies, which were set in card mounts printed with the company name and usually sold in sets of eight. Hard to imagine today, but the slides sold like hotcakes in their shop, resulting in a drop in magazine sales. I guess the slides being in colour made the images more realistic and potentially lifesize when projected on a wall. Compared to what is available on the internet today, it's hard to see what all the fuss was about. At least the models back then were all natural – no facelifts, no silicone: real women.

Working in the office, I became great friends with Pam and George. At the time, the Harrison Marks empire was going from strength to strength. Mail order was booming, and I would sometimes go to the post office, which was at the other end of the street, twice a day. It was difficult to keep up with demand. Mrs Green, Pamela's mum, would often help out in the office during busy periods. George was a family-oriented man. He would often employ the boyfriends and husbands of the staff who worked there. It brought a certain sort of closeness and loyalty to the whole enterprise.

Searching for a way to expand the business further, George started making 8mm strip films. The first one, *Art for Arts Sake* (1960), starred Pam and me. Pamela's mum even got involved with the films, playing the occasional extra, such as the landlady in *A Flat Spin* (1960), which starred Mary Deighan. With George's attention elsewhere, the quality of the slides began to deteriorate. The early sets were themed and curated, while the later ones were increasingly just mixed sets of random images. The newer and cheaper film stock meant the colours were prone to fading. And the little red boxes were replaced with clear plastic wallets.

I continued with the photographic modelling and working in the office until 1962. Looking back and reminiscing about working in London's Soho in the late fifties and early sixties, I can't help feeling what a wonderful and special time it was. But maybe that was because we were young.

Jean Spaul, 2021

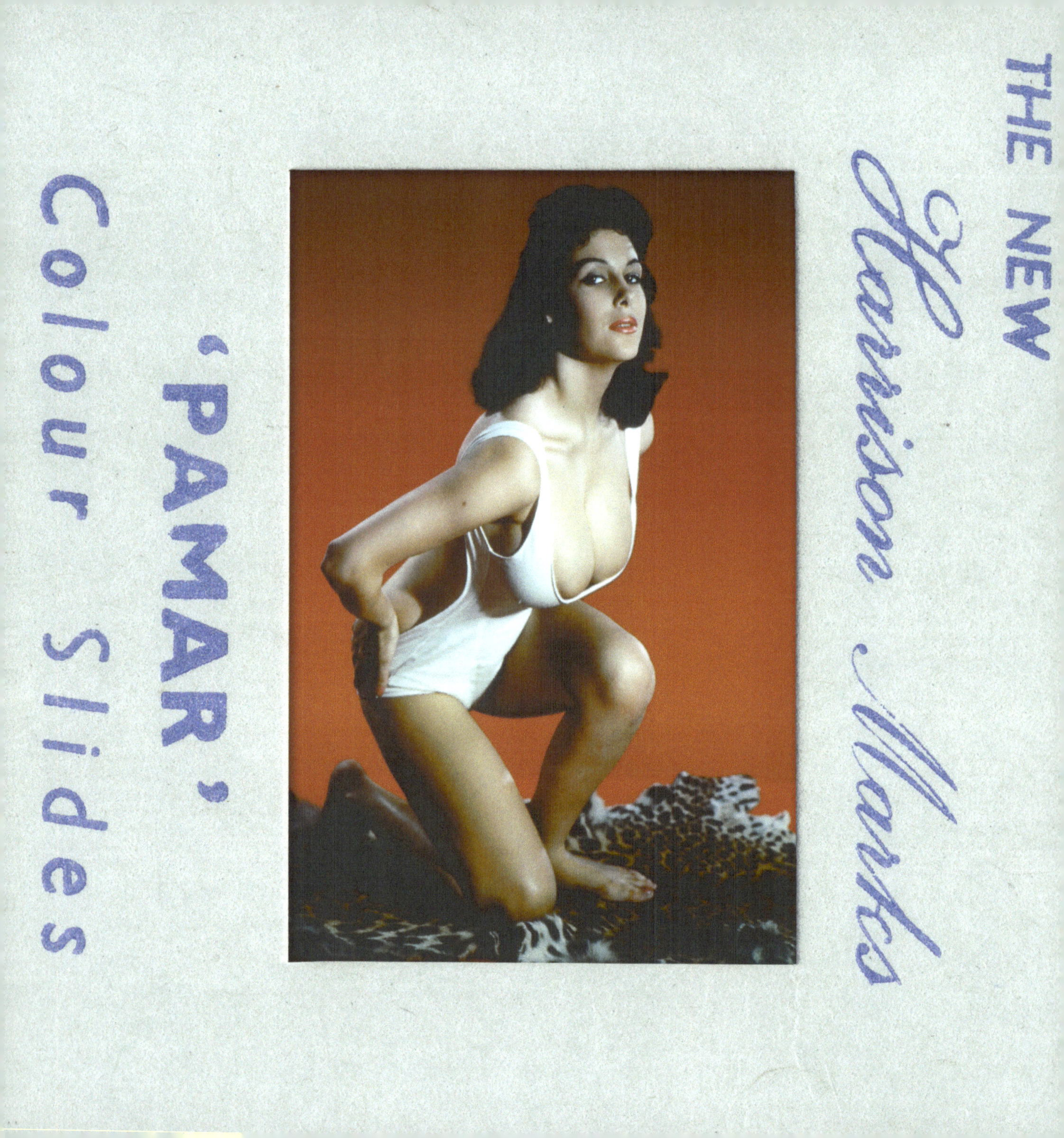

THE NEW
Harrison Marks
'PAMAR'
Colour Slides

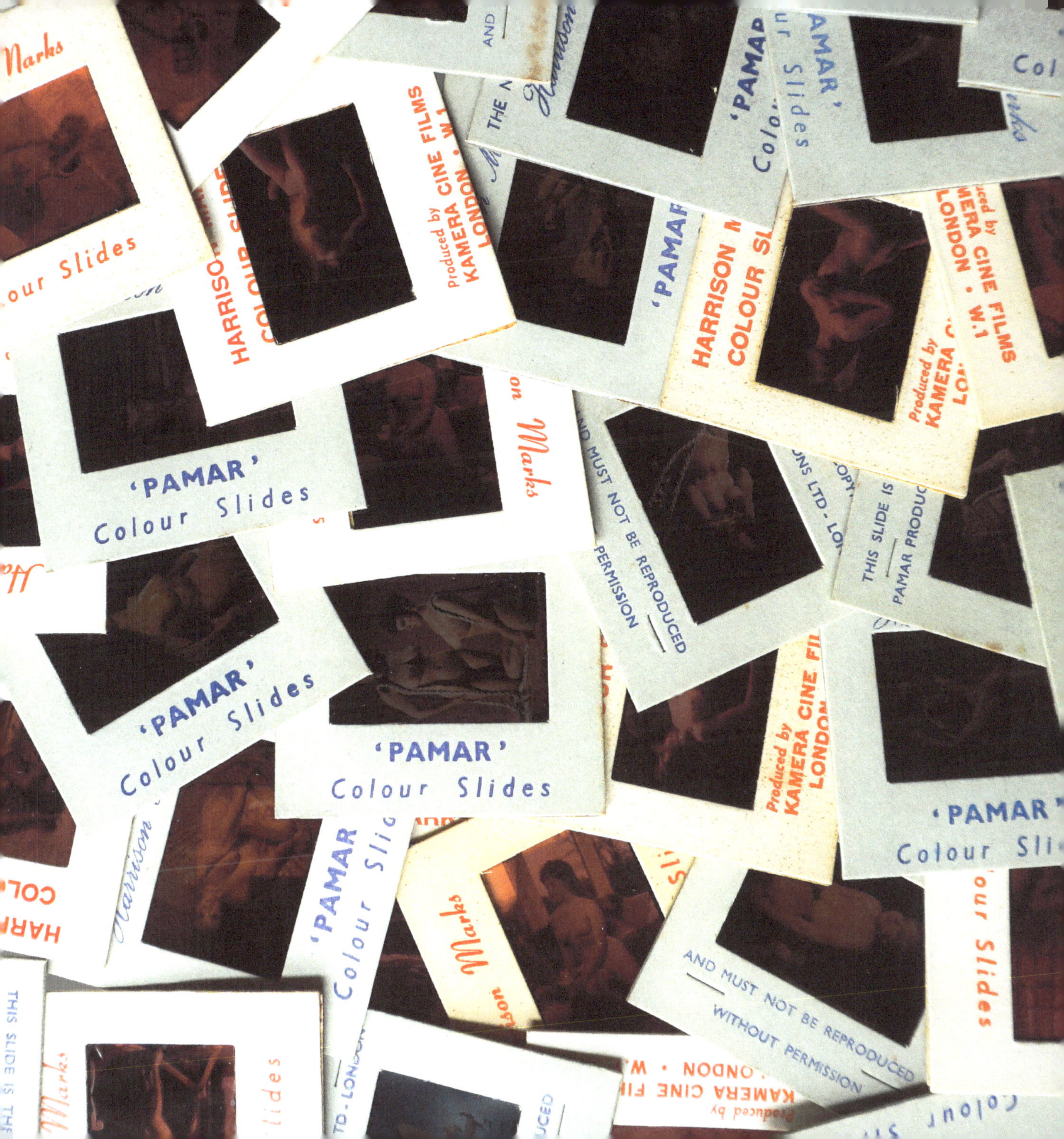
'PAMAR'
Colour Slides
HARRISON
COLOUR SLIDES
Produced by KAMERA CINE FILMS
LONDON • W.1
Marks
AND MUST NOT BE REPRODUCED
WITHOUT PERMISSION
THIS SLIDE IS
PAMAR PRODUC

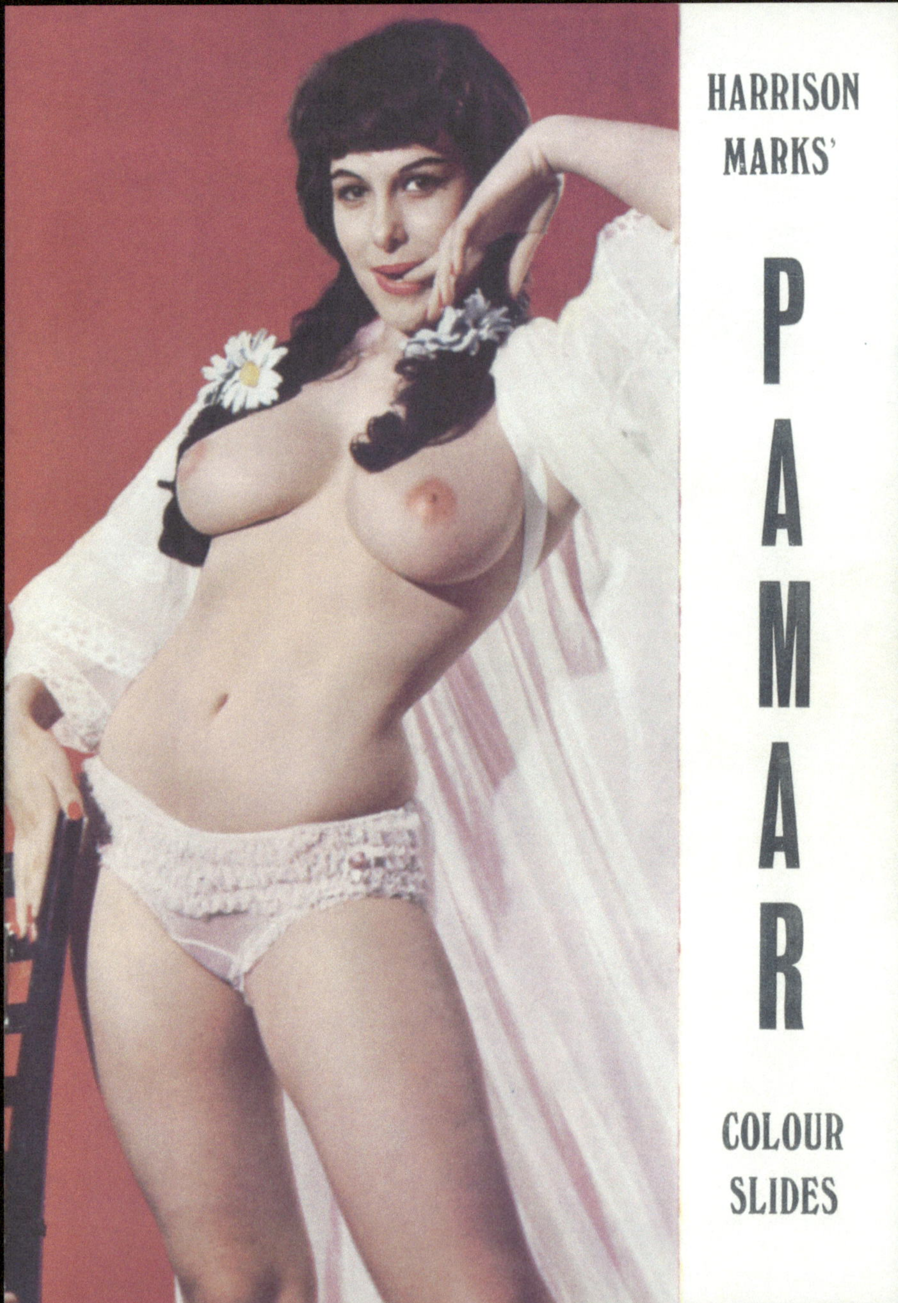
HARRISON
MARKS'
PAMAR
COLOUR
SLIDES

PAMAR COLOUR SLIDES

FABULOUS ERICA

Who can doubt this statement? With measurements of 44-24-39. this magnificent model has modelled for a series of colour sets which will delight and astound the viewer.

No. 1 8 Slides. Nudes in and around the flat
No. 2 8 Slides. A further series in the same setting
No. 3 8 Slides. In the dressing room
No. 4 8 Slides. In a further dressing room series
No. 5 8 Slides. Fascinating and unusual
No. 6 8 Slides. In a magnificent attic moonlit setting
No. 7 8 Slides. Nude and lingerie studies in an artist's attic
No. 8 12 Slides. Featuring Erica on stage doing an actual striptease

PAT DAVIS

A new model with a 44 bust measurement – truly one of the most magnificent figure lines photographed. The three sets presented all show this model at her loveliest.

No. 9 12 Slides. A wonderful series in and around an artist's garrett
No. 10 12 Studies in relaxed mood at home
No. 11 12 further studies in the same setting

THELMA

A beautiful Jamaican model, featured in two series of studies at home and in the studio.

No. 12 8 Slides in studio
No. 12 8 Slides at home

DIANA HEDGES

A beautiful series of this popular model in an informal set of slides in and around the apartment.

No. 14 12 Slides

THERESE SEYMOURE

Has been described as one of London's most perfect models. We agree, as we know you will when you view this set of magnificent slides.

No. 15 8 Slides

ROSEMARY AND BRIDGET

Two beautiful new models: Rosemary, a lovely English girl, and Bridget, a petit French model. Posed in a colourful attic setting.

No. 16 12 Slides

JENNIFER GARLAND

By the number of sets we are running, you will realise the high opinion we hold of this wonderful model. Her flaming red hair and fabulous measurements make Jennifer one of the most Glamourous girls we have ever used.

No. 17 8 Slides in the Dressing Room
No. 18 8 Slides in a further series in the same setting
No. 19 A Series of 8 wonderful figure studies
No. 20 8 Terrific studies in a backstage setting
No. 21 8 Studies in studio settings
No. 22 A unique series of 12 studies in various moods and settings

ROSA

A Top figure model with magnificent measurements, known to all collectors of photographic art. We have pleasure in including her in our new series.

No. 23 8 Studies in an informal home setting
No. 24 8 Slides in a further "at home" selection
No. 25 8 Studies in a "record" figure collection

JUNE SIMPSON

A poem of line in every limb is how we describe this magnificent, acrobatic figure model.

No. 26 8 Slides in a series of studio settings
No. 27 12 Slides showing the fantastic versatility of this wonderful lithe model

LORRAINE BURNETT

Cute, effervescent, beautiful. How else can we describe one of the most popular models we have ever photographed. All three sets are featured in an "at home" setting, guaranteed to delight the viewer.

No. 28 8 Slides
No. 29 8 Slides
No. 30 8 Slides

ANN AUSTIN

Need we say more, except to say that in all the Feminine attributes she rates 10 out of 10 on our list.

No. 31 8 Studies in a mixed studio setting
No. 32 8 Slides featuring Ann at home
No. 33 A further 8 Studies in the same setting
No. 34 12 Fabulous Figure Studies in an unusual hayloft setting
No. 35 12 Figure Studies in an Apache street scene: unusual, provocative and appealing

MADELAINE MADO

Britain's answer to B.B. of the French Cinema. If it can be said that sex appeal is the main factor for stardom, this beautiful girl is a star in the making.

No. 36 8 Slides in a boudoir series
No. 37 8 Slides featuring a cute studio series

MARY DEIGHAN

A pixyish Irish colleen whose charm and figure has rocketed her to the top of the modelling profession. These two series are a delight in Form and Colour.

No. 38 8 Slides featuring a studio mixture
No. 39 A Fabulous set of 12 studies in a theatrical setting

JUNE RUSSELL

The essence of a classical Figure model. We are proud to include this beautiful studio series in our collection.

No. 40 8 Slides

JULIE SHEARING

The full beauty of colour is captured in the series of this lovely model, who is now making a name for herself in T.V. A welcome addition to the series.

No. 41 A series of 12 wonderful studies of mixed studies
No. 42 12 Studies in and around the model's flat

PAMELA GREEN & MARIE DEVERAUX

Here is a series of 8 studies of extreme beauty featuring two of Britain's Greatest Models.

No. 43 8 Slides in studio settings

PAMELA GREEN & JUNE SIMPSON

Again we present a series featuring two top models, this time in a wonderful summer-house setting.

No. 44 8 Slides

ROSA, LORRAINE & MAXINE

Three of our most popular models, brought together in one set of studio studies

No. 45 12 Slides

DRESSING ROOM SERIES

Here is a really beautiful set of informal shots showing the models illustrated Nude and in lingerie.

No. 46 8 Slides

MARIE DEVERAUX

We present the last Figure & Pin-up studies of this lovely girl, taken just before she became a Film Starlet. Filmdom's gain is our loss.

No. 47 8 Various studies in studio settings
No. 48 8 Further studies in the studio
No. 49 8 Slides of Marie in and around the flat
No. 50 8 Beautiful Figure studies in a Fisher-girl setting

VANDA HUDSON

A beautiful series of studies featuring the Film & T.V. Star: no other series available anywhere.

No. 51 8 Slides

CAROL

Here is a series featuring the model so popular in our Location Colour Series. This time featured in the studio on Black Velvet.

No. 52 8 Studies

THE FABULOUS–THE UNIQUE! RITA LANDRE

There is no need to advertise Britain's Queen of Glamour. If you've already seen her pictures, we know you will eventually purchase the whole series.

No. 53 8 Mixed Studio Studies
No. 54 8 Slides as a Fisher-girl (illustrated)
No. 55 12 Terrific Slides, nude & lingerie in Parisienne and Studio sets
No. 56 12 Slides amidst the glamour of Satin Sheets
No. 57 12 Delightfully informal studies around the house

BRITAIN'S TOP MODEL! PAMELA GREEN

So much has been written and said of this magnificent beauty, that it is impossible for us to say anything new. Sufficient to say that in any of the following 5 sets, you will see Figure modelling at its greatest – by the greatest.

No. 58 8 Slides in an attic boudoir
No. 59 8 Slides entitled "Taking a bath"
No. 60 A Series of 12 studies in and around the house
No. 61 12 Delightfully tantalising slides featuring Pam as a Parisienne Flower Girl

PAMELA & JEAN SPAUL

No. 62 12 wonderful pictures of two wonderful models, featured together in various "at home" settings

JEAN SPAUL

In the following three series, we present studies of one of the most perfect models in this country. We are proud to be able to offer these exclusive slides.

No. 63 8 Slides of Jean at home
No. 64 8 Studies in the nude, presenting Jean as a beggar girl on the streets of Paris
No. 65 8 Slides entitled "Penthouse"

PRINCESS SONMAR HARRIKS

If you don't know now, you never will ? ? ? ?

No. 66 8 Slides presenting the Fantastic Dance of the Veils
No. 67 8 Wonderfully coloured slides in a studio setting
No. 68 12 Slides featured in an artist's attic
No. 69 12 Studies in a hayloft

MIXED SERIES

We follow here with a series of 12 sets designed to please all – each set contains 12 studies, all completely different, featuring different models.

Set Nos: 70, 71, 72, 73, 74, 75, 76, 77, 78, 79.

DIANE CLARE

The only recent studies of this popular model taken. In these delightful colour studies, we feature Diane in an unusual artist's attic setting.

No. 80 8 Studies in an attic boudoir
No. 81 12 Slides featuring Diane in an attic "bric-a-brac" setting

KAMERA BACKSTAGE

32 slides of the HARRISON MARKS MODELS in a backstage theatre setting. Why go to Paris? Here is a complete nude show which you can carry around in your pocket. For the entire set in its own presentation box we have made a specially reduced price.

Printed in England by Martins Press Ltd., London, S.E.1

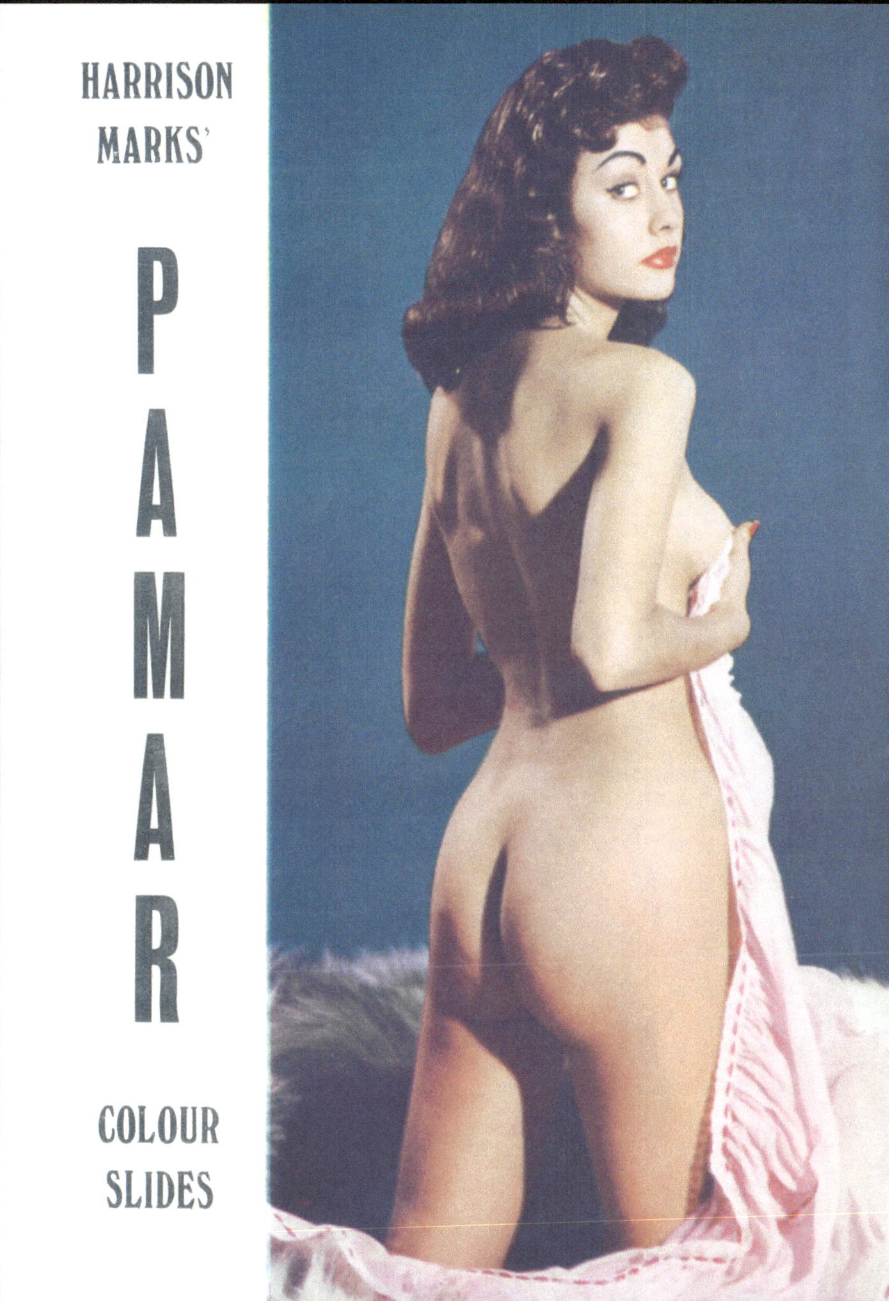
HARRISON
MARKS'
PAMAR
COLOUR
SLIDES

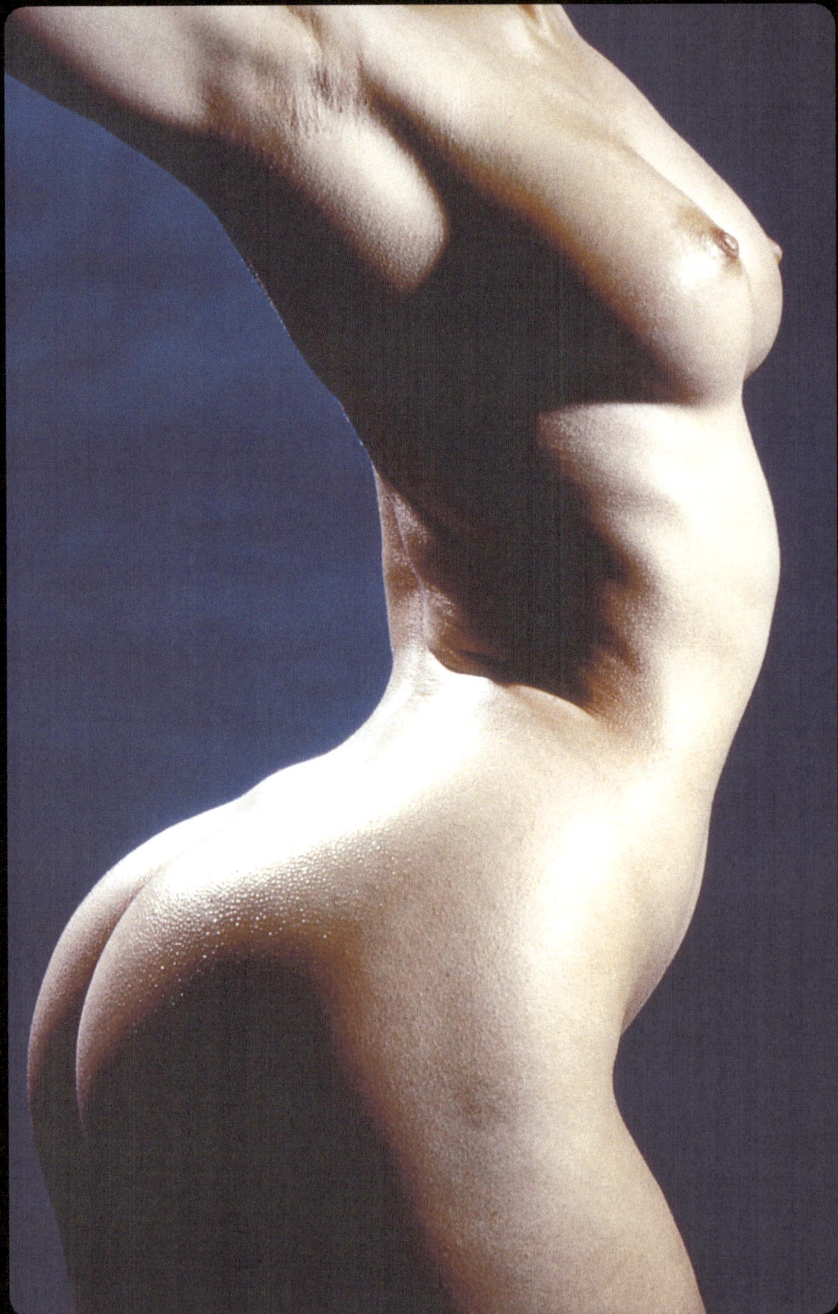

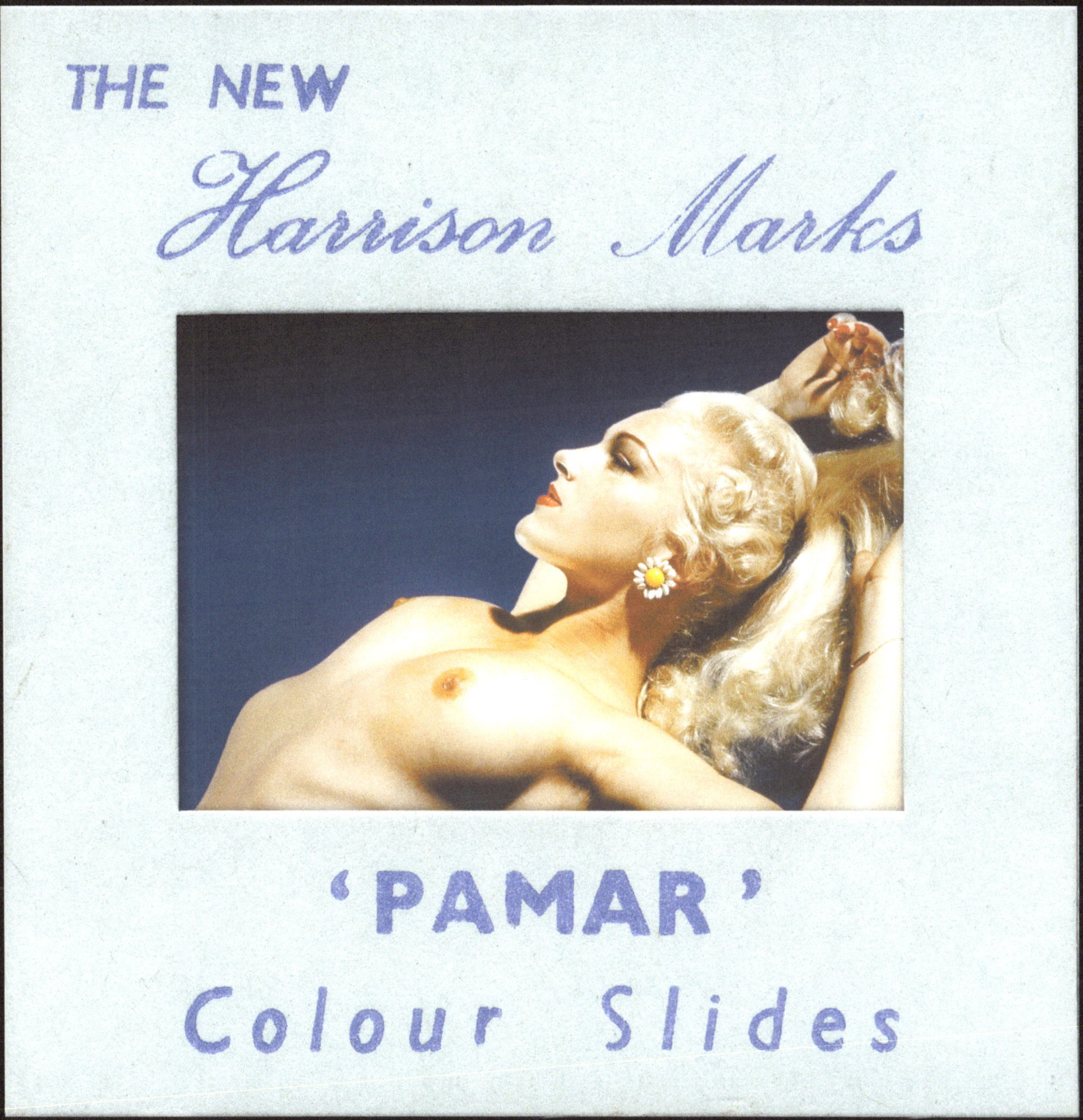
THE NEW
Harrison Marks
'PAMAR'
Colour Slides

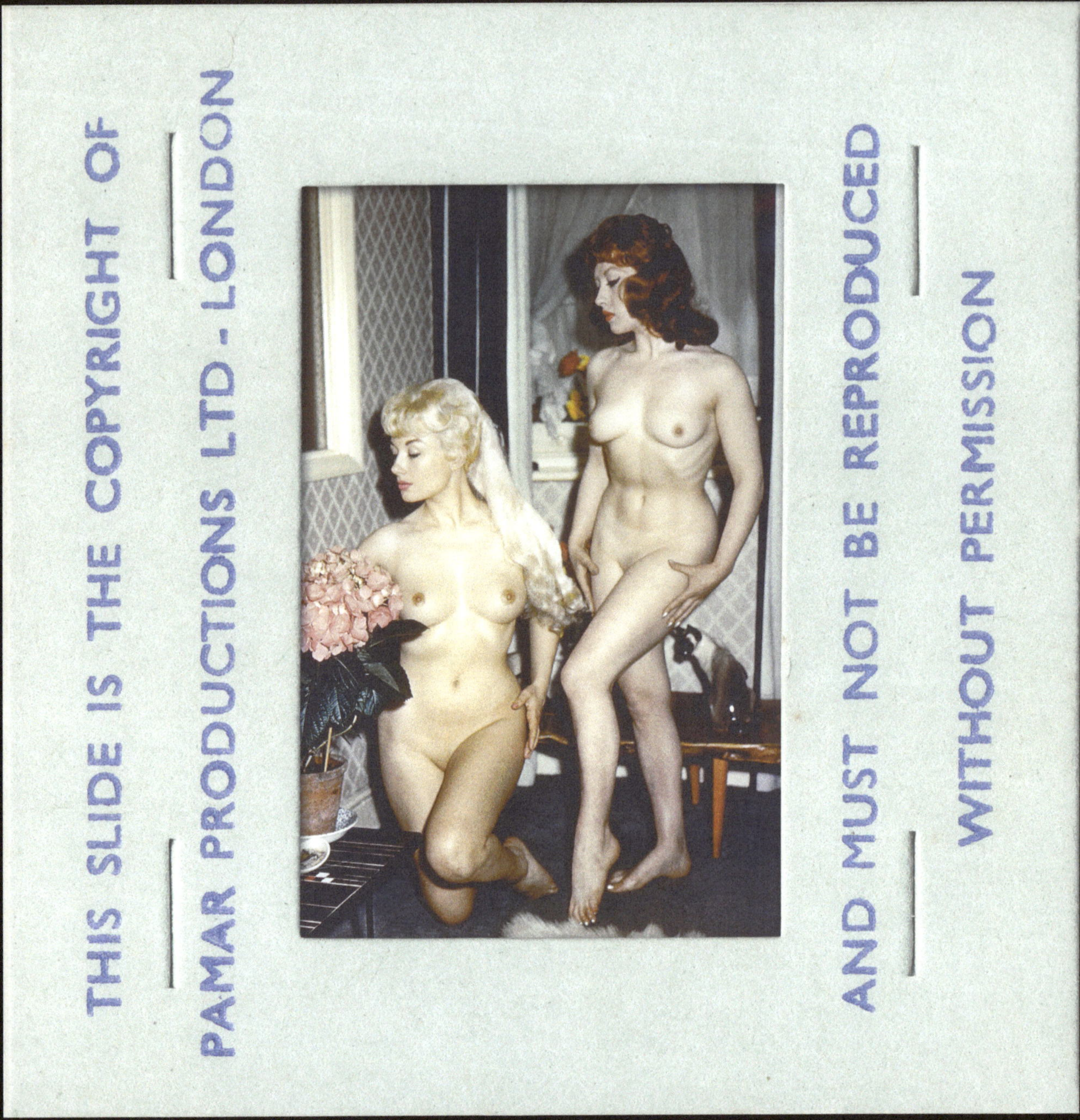
THIS SLIDE IS THE COPYRIGHT OF
PAMAR PRODUCTIONS LTD - LONDON
AND MUST NOT BE REPRODUCED
WITHOUT PERMISSION

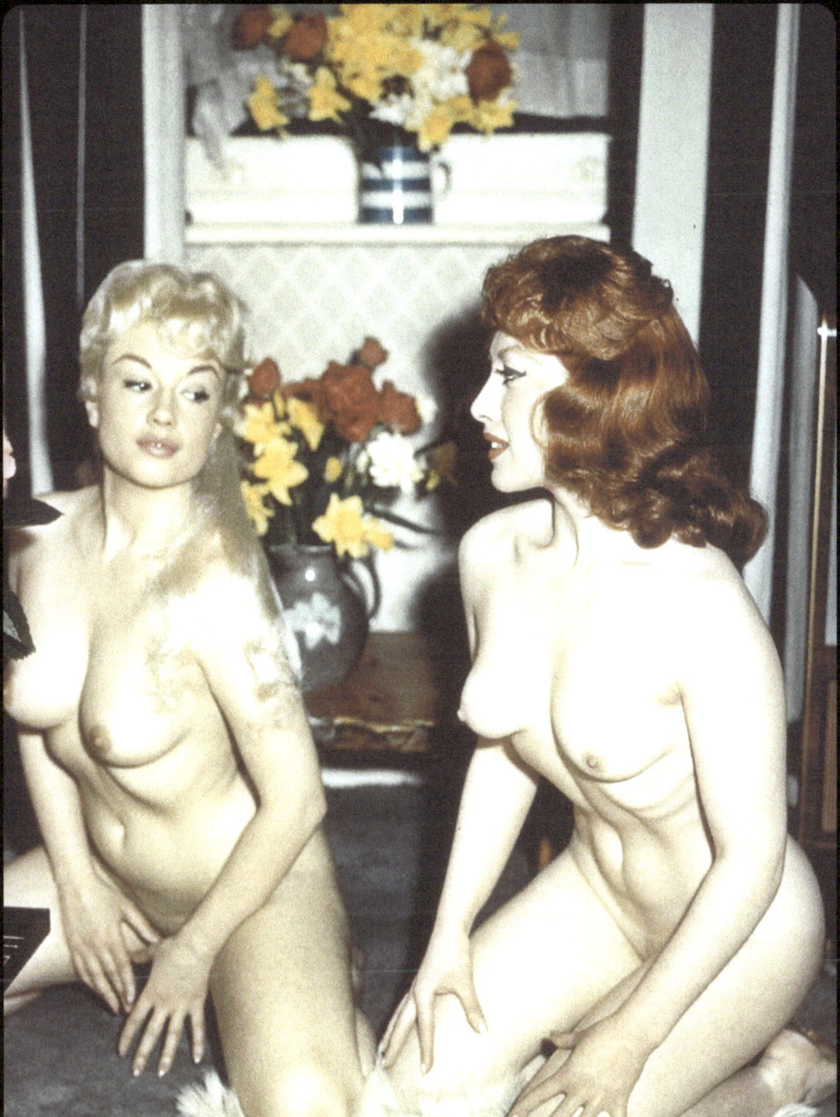

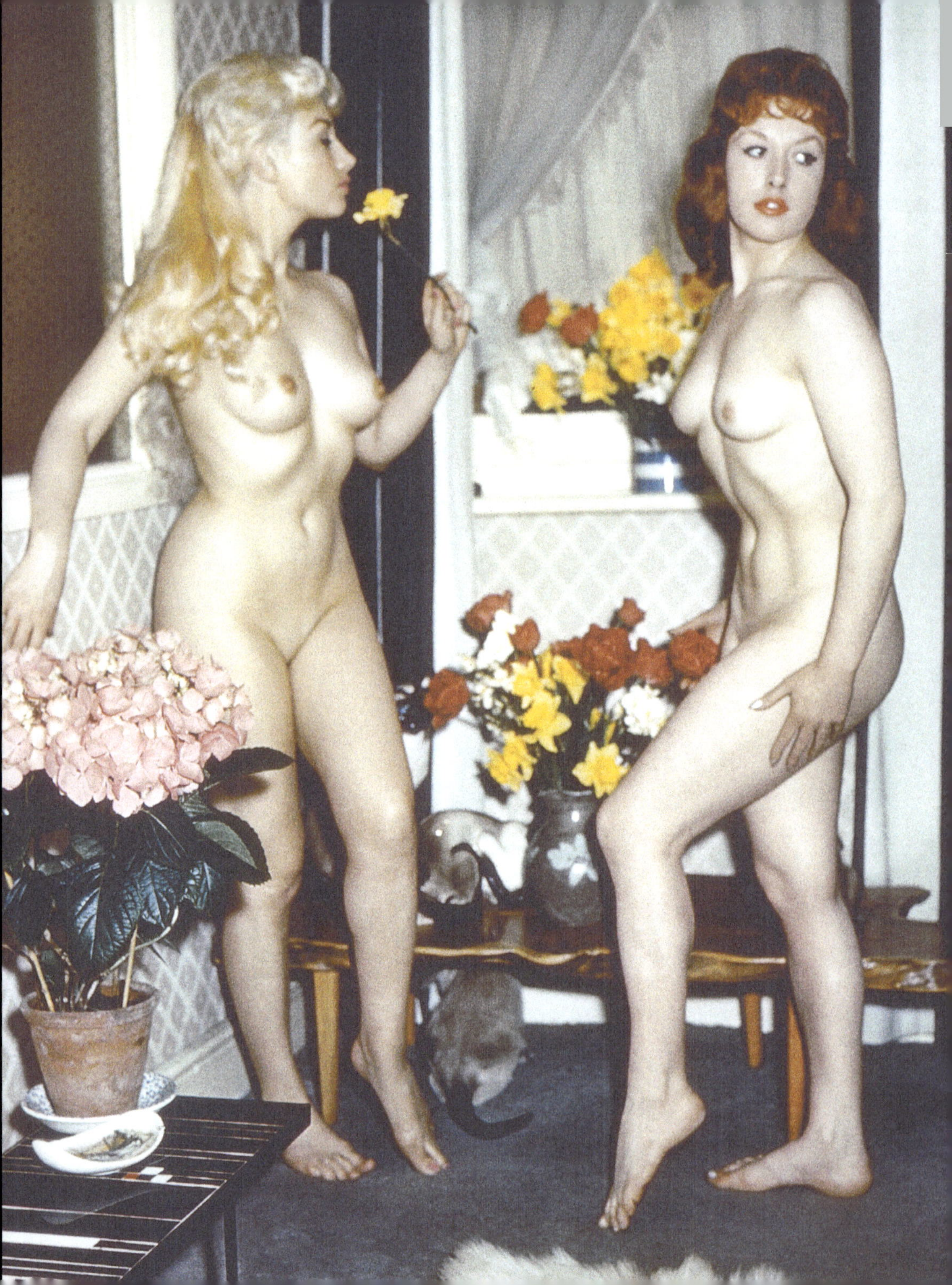

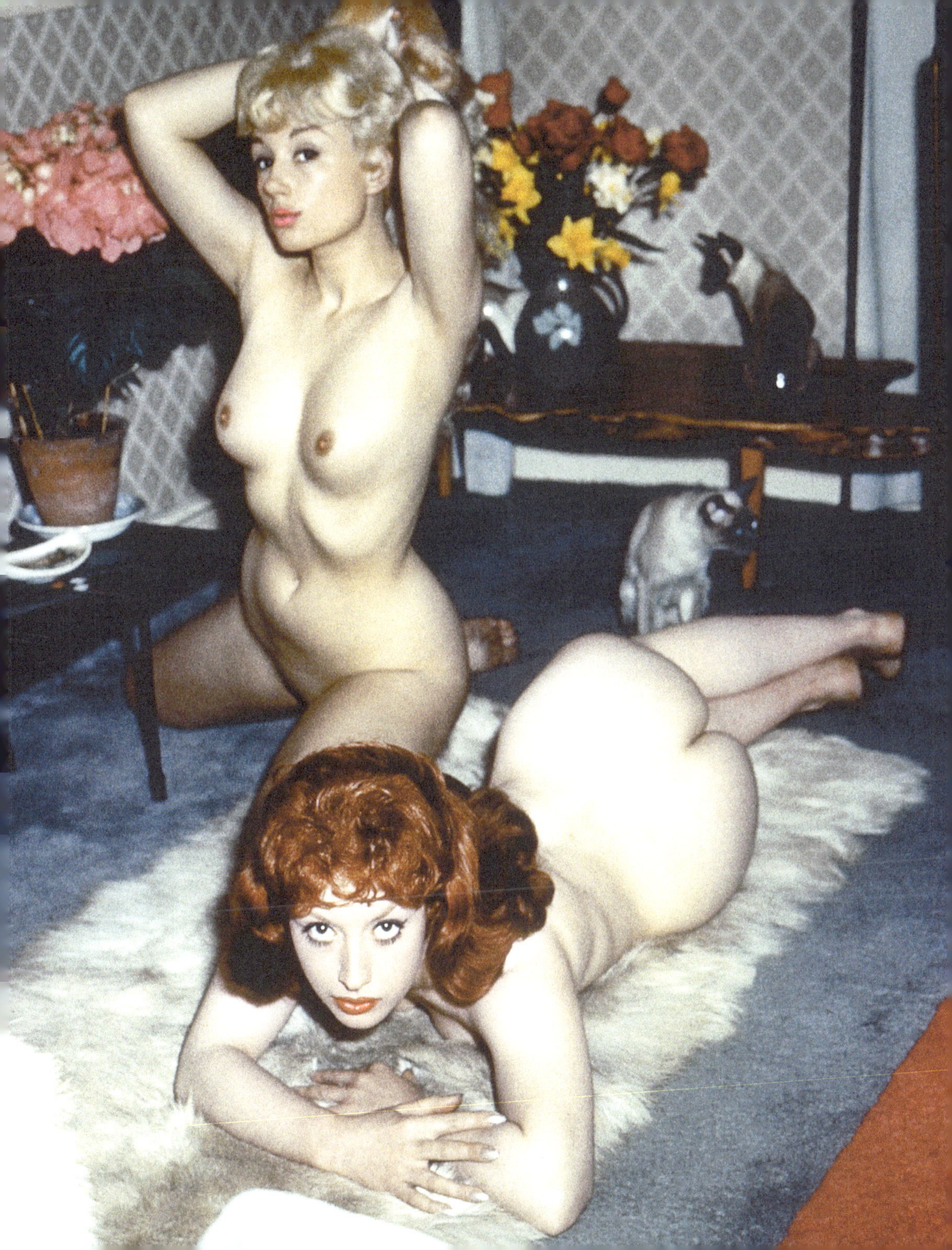

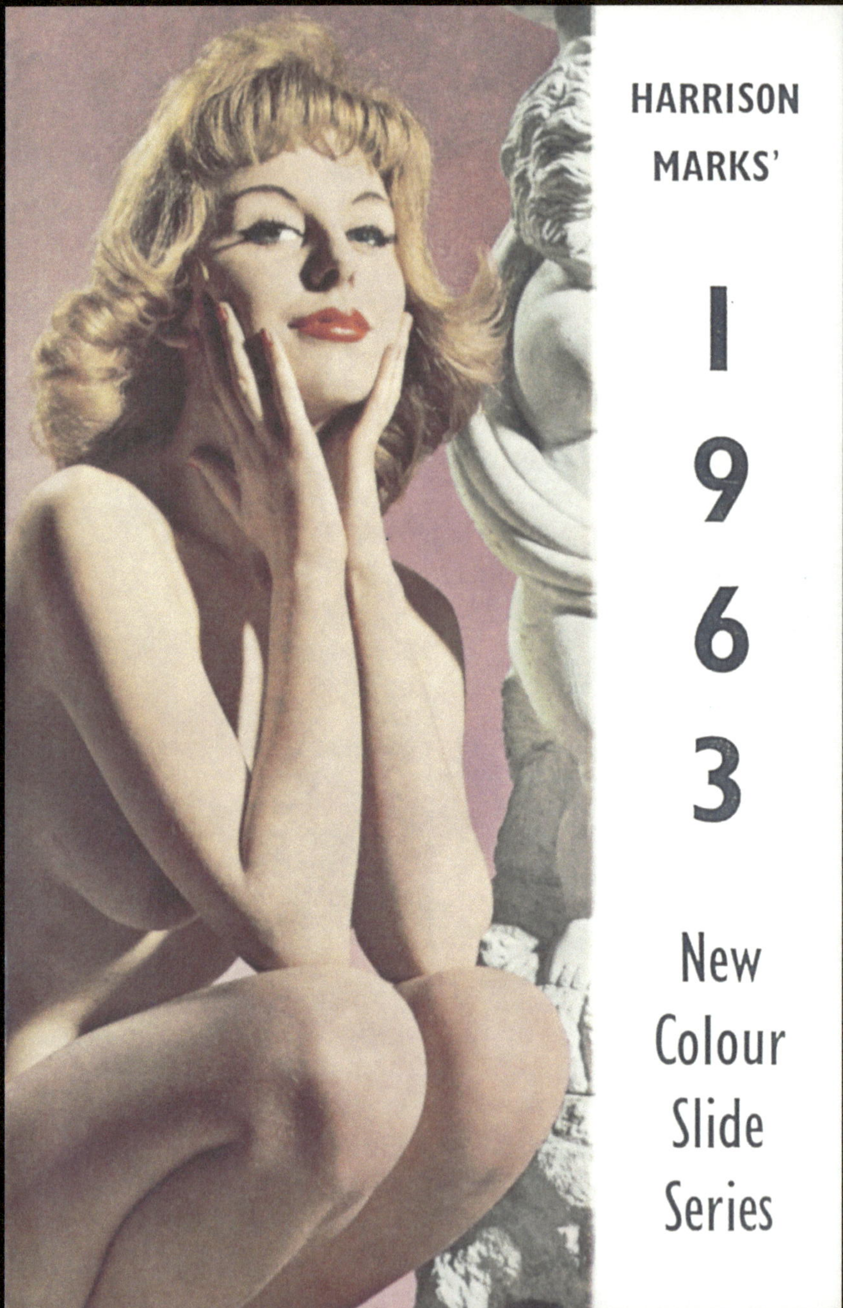
HARRISON
MARKS'
1
9
6
3
New
Colour
Slide
Series

HARRISON MARKS COLOUR SLIDES

Pamela Green and Harrison Marks formed Pamar Productions Ltd in June 1957. When their personal relationship ended in the early sixties, Pamela continued as a director of Kamera Publications and Pamar Productions Ltd, but as time went on, she became less involved with the businesses. This resulted in George using the company Kamera Cine Films to produce any new sets of slides, which he then labelled "Harrison Marks Colour Slides". Seventy-two sets were produced. Frustratingly for collectors, the sets were very easy to muddle up, and over the years, they have been broken down and the slides sold individually.

Set 1 8 slides including: Tina Graham, Lorraine Burnett, Angela Jones, June Palmer

Set 2 8 slides including: June Simpson, Pamela Green, Kay Fitzsimmons, Christine Scott

Set 3 A complete set of Tina Graham

Set 4 8 slides including: Jennifer Garland, Mary Deigham, Ann Austin, Maria Hale

Set 5 8 slides including: Marie Deveraux, Maxine, Virginia Green, Jean Spaul

Set 6 8 slides including: Avra Bennett, Paula Page, Jaki Salt, Tina Graham

Set 7 8 slides including: Erica Angela Jones, Pamela Green, Jean Spaul, Paula Page

Set 8 8 slides including: Madelaine Mills, Terry Peters, June Palmer, Christine Scott

Set 9 8 slides including: Erica Angela Jones, Kay Fitzsimmons, Pamela Green

Set 10 A complete set of Pamela Green

Set 11 8 slides including: Rusty Gaynor, Jayne Tracy, Eve Eden, Terry Peters

Set 12 A complete set of June Palmer

Set 13 A complete set of June Palmer

Set 14 A complete set of Pamela Green

Set 15 8 slides including: Caron Gardiner, Eve Eden, Jaki Salt, Maxine

Set 16 8 slides including: Chu Chu, Deborah de Lacy, Jane Mathews, Vivienne Warren

Set 17 8 slides including: Yamille, Vicky Kennedy, Tina Graham, Ellaine Desmonde

Set 18 8 slides including: Sonmar, Bridget Leonard, Rita Landre, Angela Jones

Set 19 8 slides including: Ann Walker, Ellaine Desmonde, Maxine, Jane Mathews

Set 20 8 slides including: Jayne Tracy, Vivienne Warren, Vicky Kennedy, June Palmer

Set 21 8 slides including: Rusty Gaynor, Sonmar, Vivienne Warren, Bridget Leonard

Set 22 8 slides including: Madelaine Mills, Angela Jones, Ellaine Desmonde, Deborah de Lacy

Set 23 8 slides including: Lorraine Burnett, Maria Clarence, Ann Walker, Jean Spaul

Set 24 8 slides including: Maria Clarence, Rusty Gaynor, Pamela Green, Jane Mathews

Set 25 8 slides including: Tina Graham, Chu Chu, Jaki Salt, Tina Madison

Set 26 A complete set of Pamela Green

Set 27 8 slides including: Yamille, Molly Peters, Maria Hale, Chu Chu

Set 28 8 slides including: Ann Austin, Ann Walker, Rusty Gaynor, Maxine

Set 29 A complete set of Vera Day

Set 30 8 slides including: Vivienne Warren, June Palmer, Pamela Green, Chu Chu

Set 31 8 slides including: Madelaine Mills, Ann Austin, Christine Scott, Terry Peters

Set 32 A complete set of Vicky Kennedy & Maria Clarence

Set 33 8 slides including: Vicky Kennedy, Rusty Gaynor, Vivienne Warren, Ann Walker

Set 34 8 slides including: Yamille, Tina Graham, Sonmar, Jaki Salt

Set 35 A complete set of Paula Page

Set 36 A complete set of Paula Page

36 New Sets

Eight exciting poses of a famous model, packed in glass-clear transparent ready view wallets.

Set 37 Sue Owen, *Beach scenes*

Set 38 Sue Owen, *Studio*

Set 39 Sue Owen, *Bedroom*

Set 40 Sue Owen, *At home*

Set 41 Hyldagarde, *At home*

Set 42 Hyldagarde, *Studio set*

Set 43 Beryl Gilchrist, *Dungeon ruins*

Set 44 Wendy Luton, *Apartment*

Set 45 Molly Peters, *At home*

Set 46 Tina McGowan, *Egyptian Temple set*

Set 47 Tina McGowan, *At home*

Set 48 Terri Martine, *Chinese set*

Set 49 Terri Martine, *Garden set*

Set 50 Ellaine Desmonde, *In woods*

Set 51 Ellaine Desmonde, *Beach scenes*

Set 52 Ann Taylor, *Bedroom*

Set 53 Cere, *Bedroom*

Set 54 Dawn Grayson, *Exterior*

Set 55 Julie Collins, *Beach scenes*

Set 56 Julie Collins, *Apartment*

Set 57 Anna Verdi, *Bedroom*

Set 58 Caroline Hughes, *Chinese garden*

Set 59 Lorraine Burnett, *Theatre dressing room*

Set 60 June Palmer, *Mixed shots*

Set 61 June Palmer, *Roman bath*

Set 62 June Palmer, *Roman set*

Set 63 Wendy James, *Studio set*

Set 64 Cleo Simmons, *Bedroom*

Set 65 Sandra Cassano, *Beach scenes*

Set 66 Sandra Cassano, *Apartment*

Set 67 Penny Winters, *Egyptian Temple set*

Set 68 Jutka Goz, *At home*

Set 69 Vera Novak, *Egyptian Temple set*

Set 70 June Johnson, *On the beach and in the flat*

Set 71 Diane James, *Egyptian Temple set*

Set 72 Vicky, *Groves Roman set*

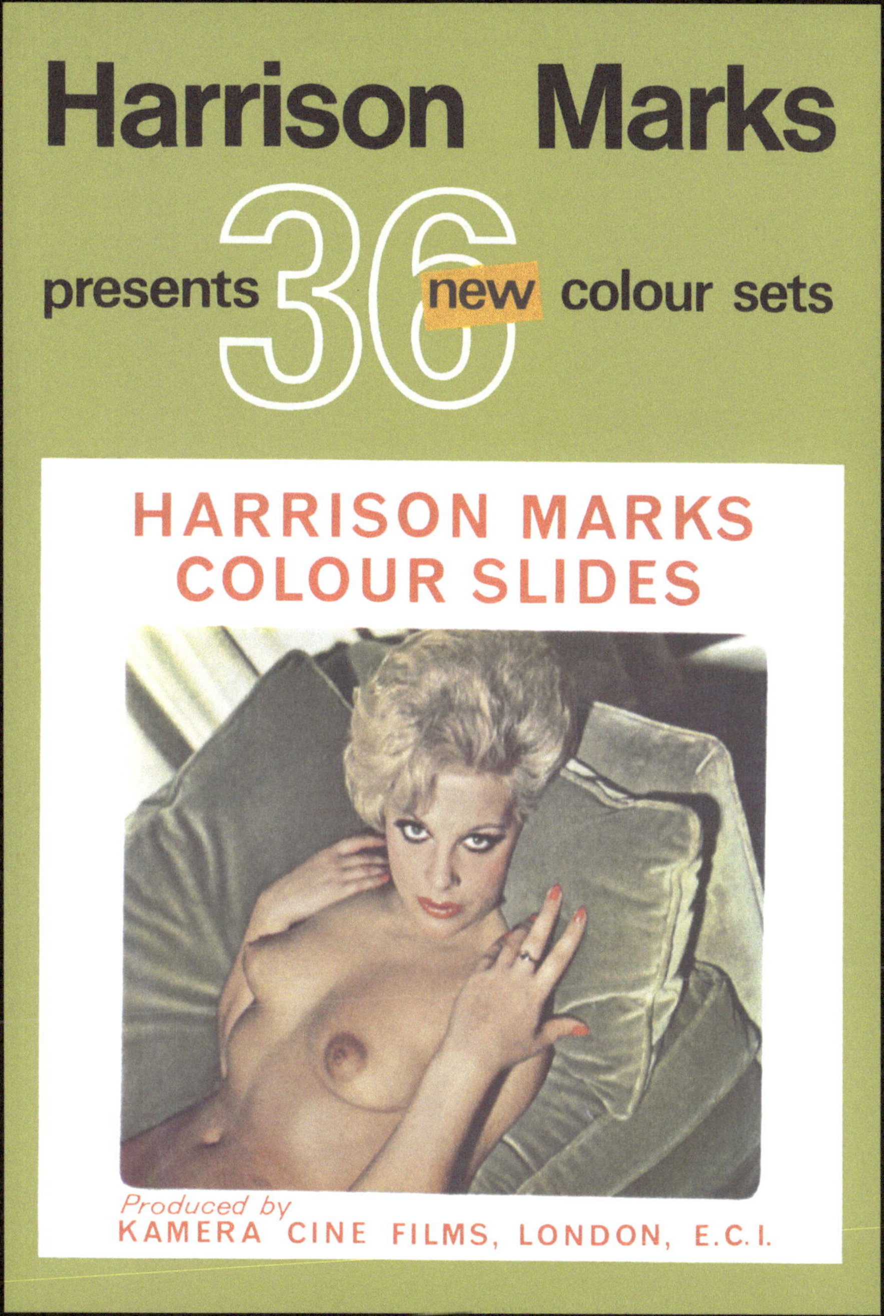
Harrison Marks
presents 36 new colour sets
HARRISON MARKS
COLOUR SLIDES
Produced by
KAMERA CINE FILMS, LONDON, E.C.1.

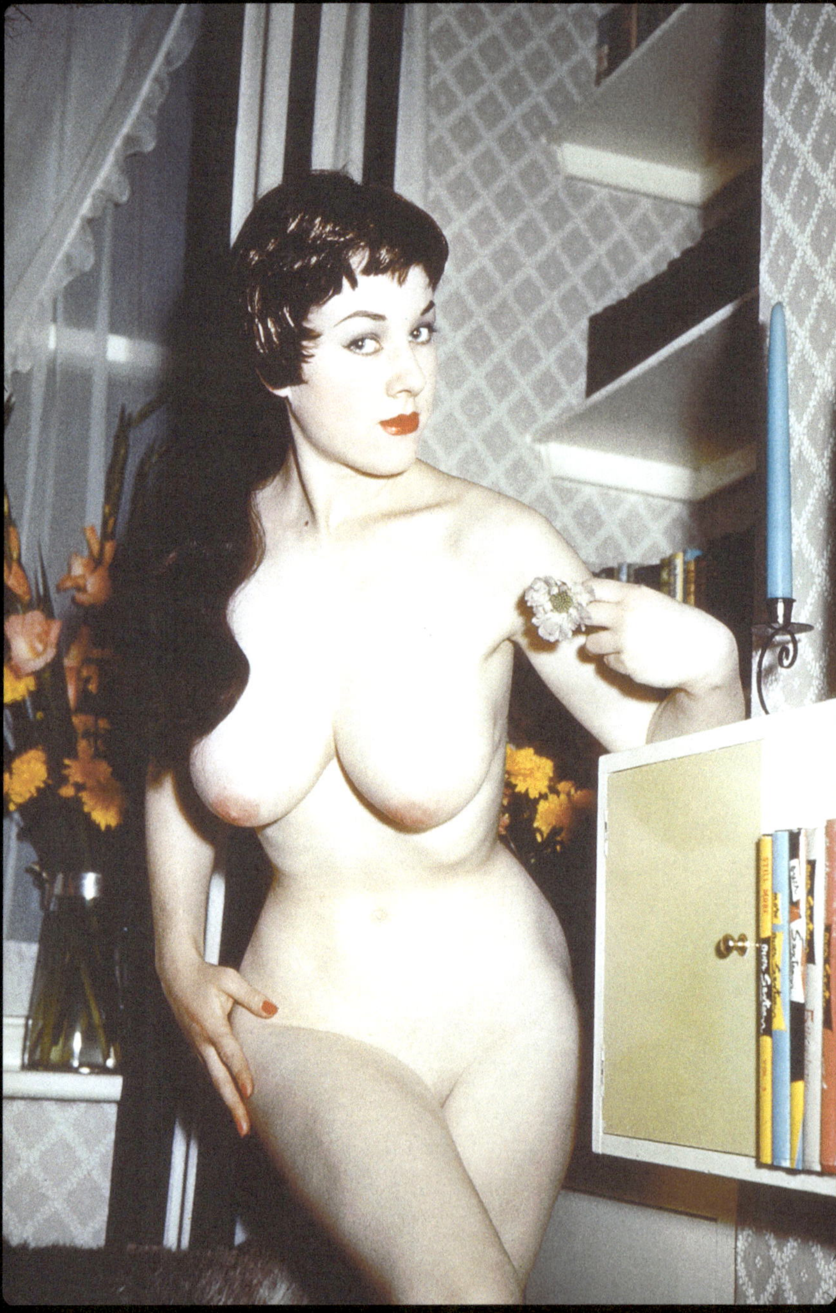

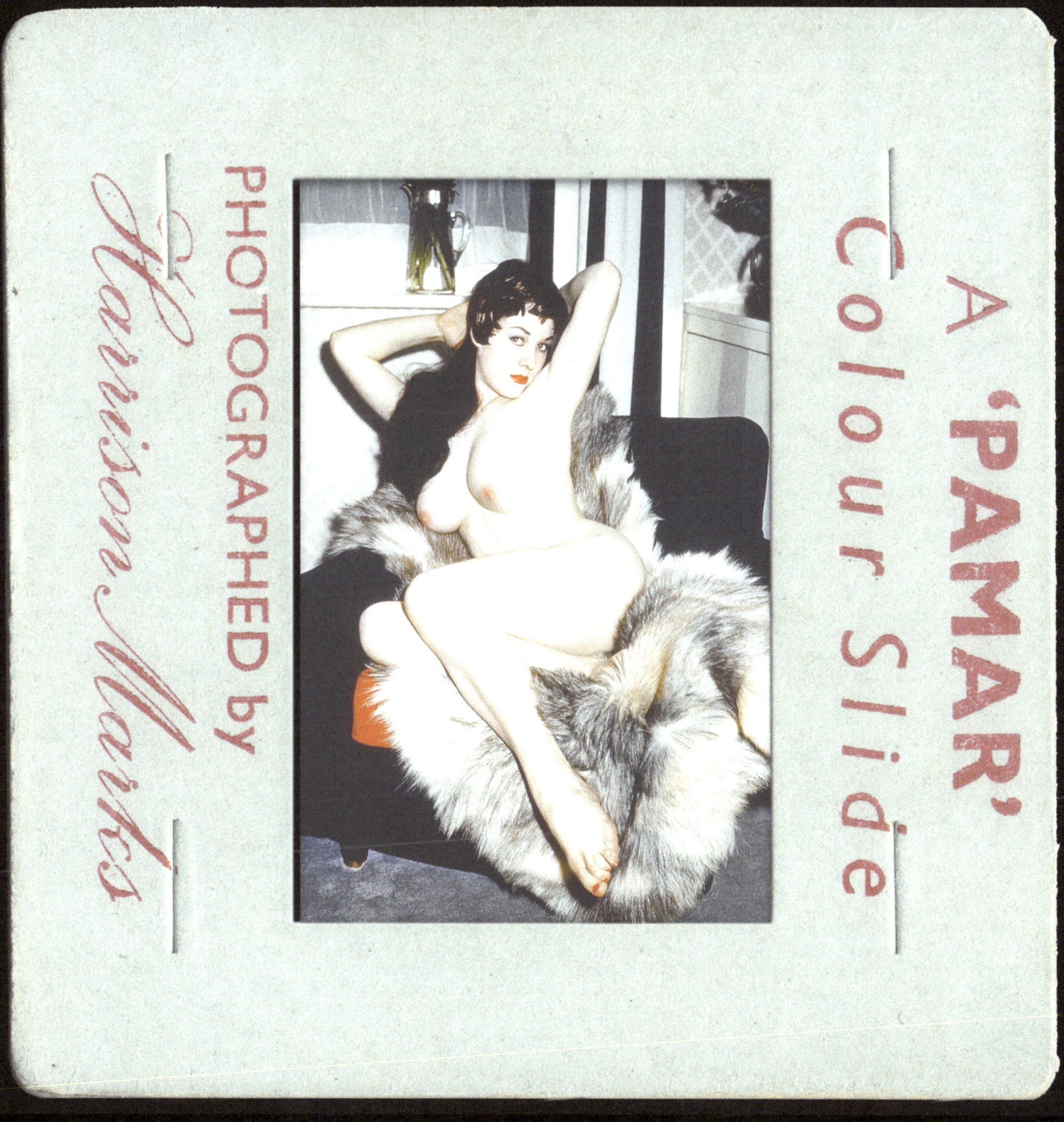
A 'PAMAR'
Colour Slide
PHOTOGRAPHED by
Harrison Marks

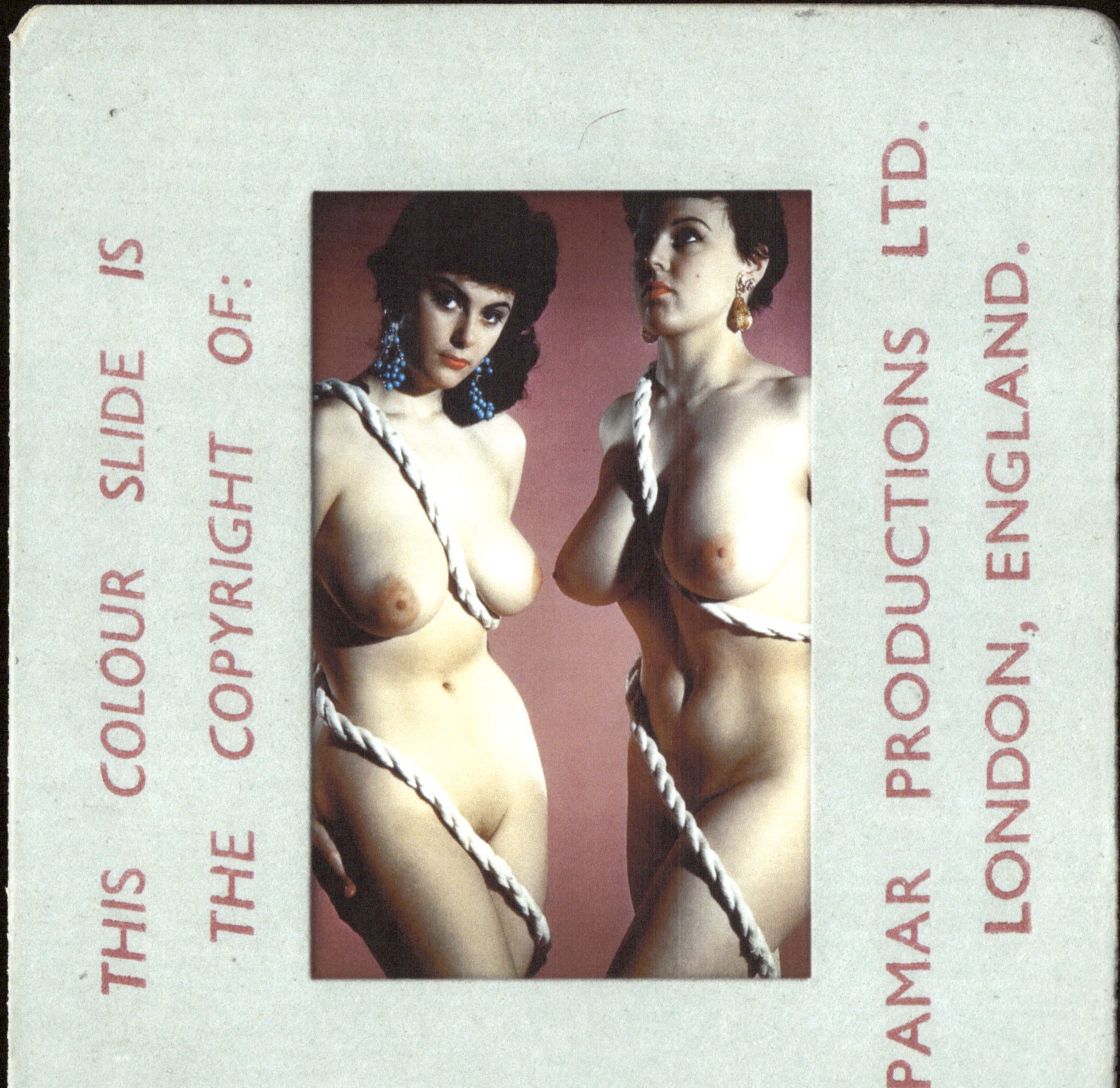
THIS COLOUR SLIDE IS
THE COPYRIGHT OF:
PAMAR PRODUCTIONS LTD.
LONDON, ENGLAND.

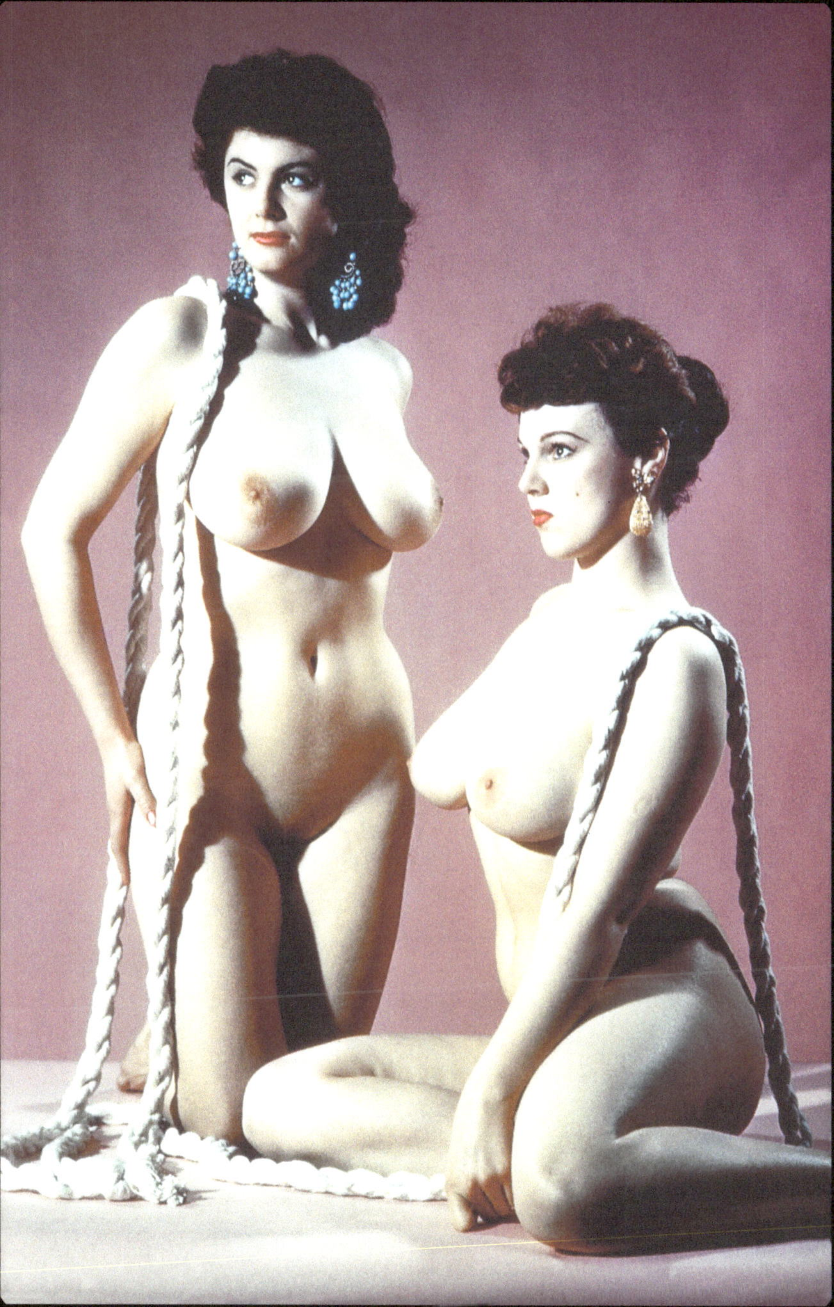

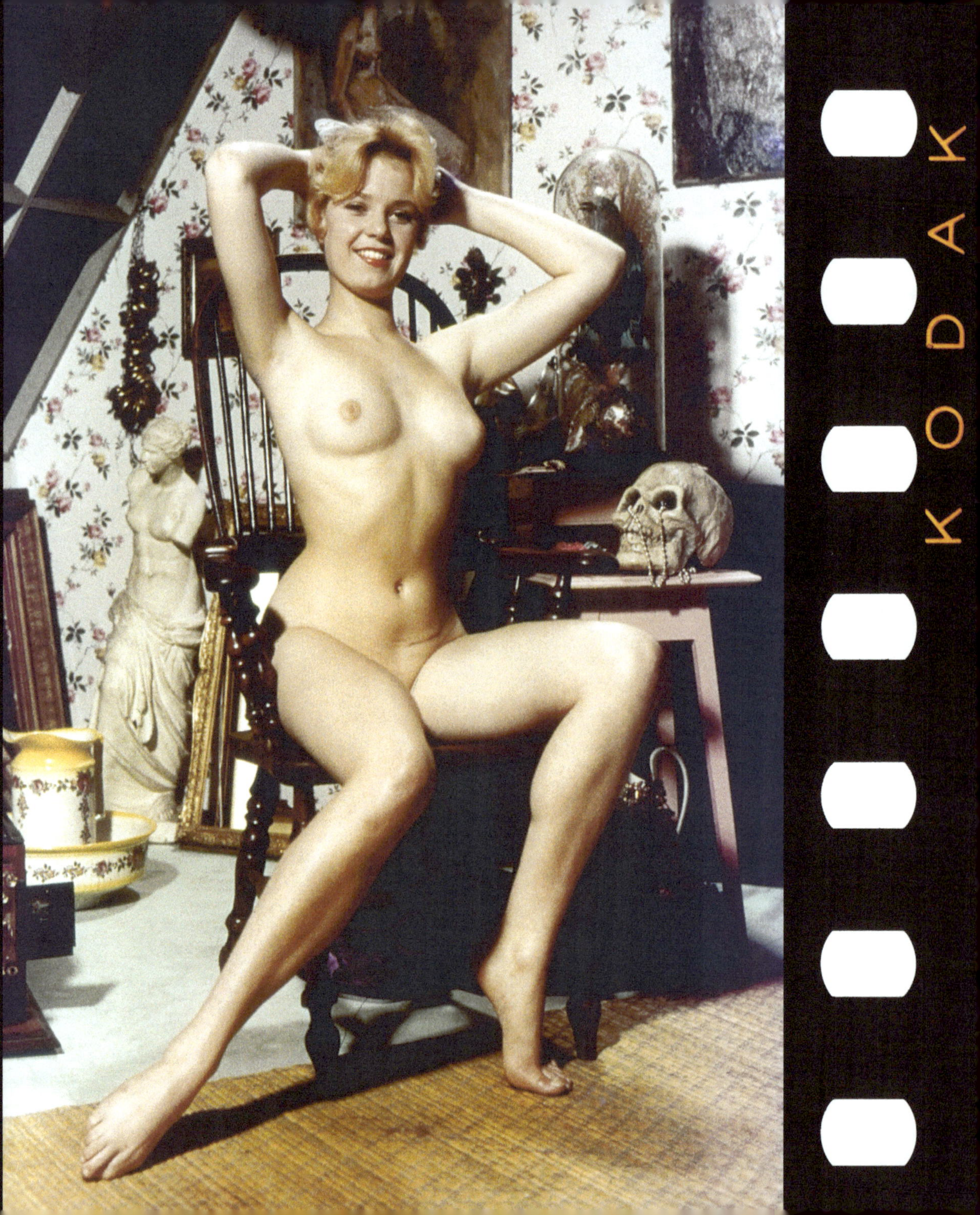
KODAK

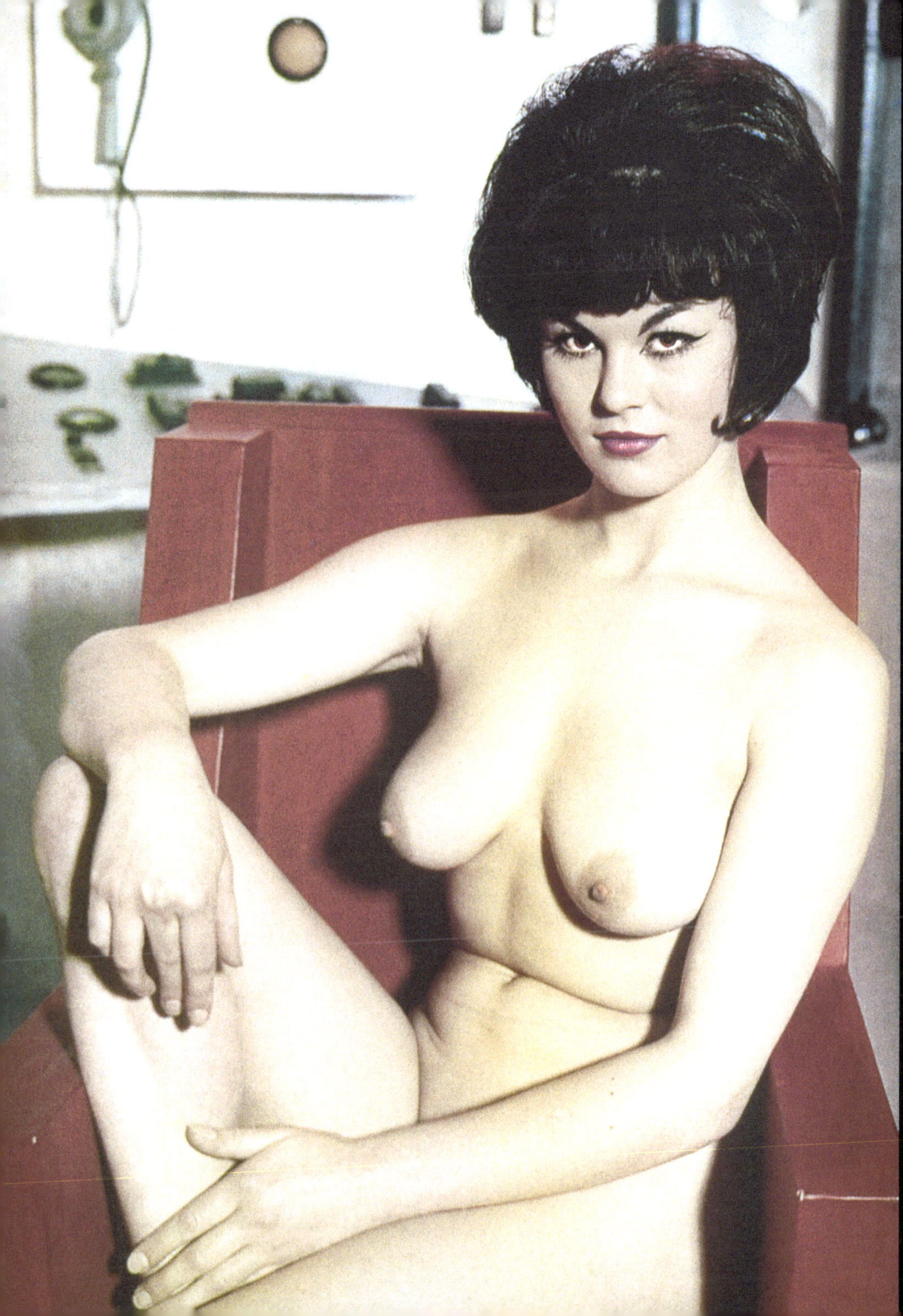

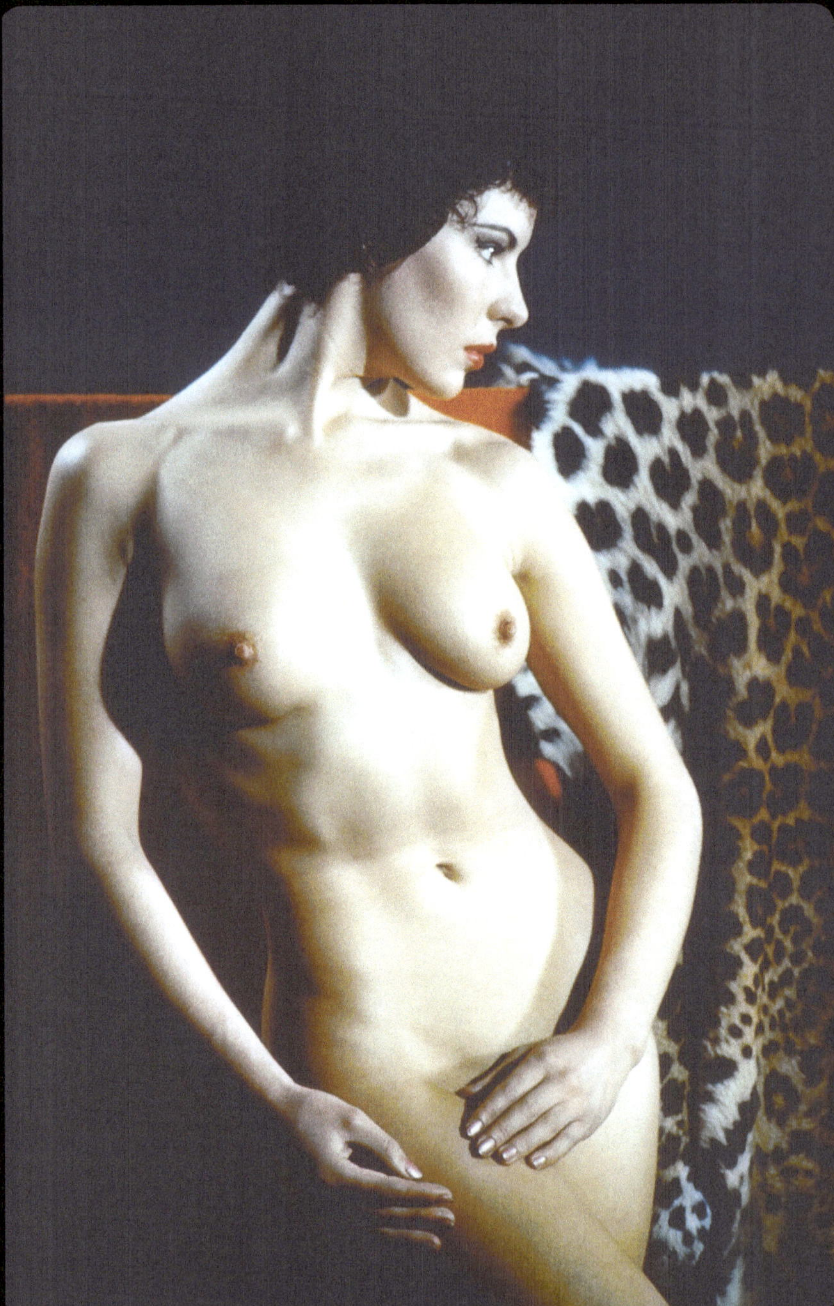

A

Harrison Marks

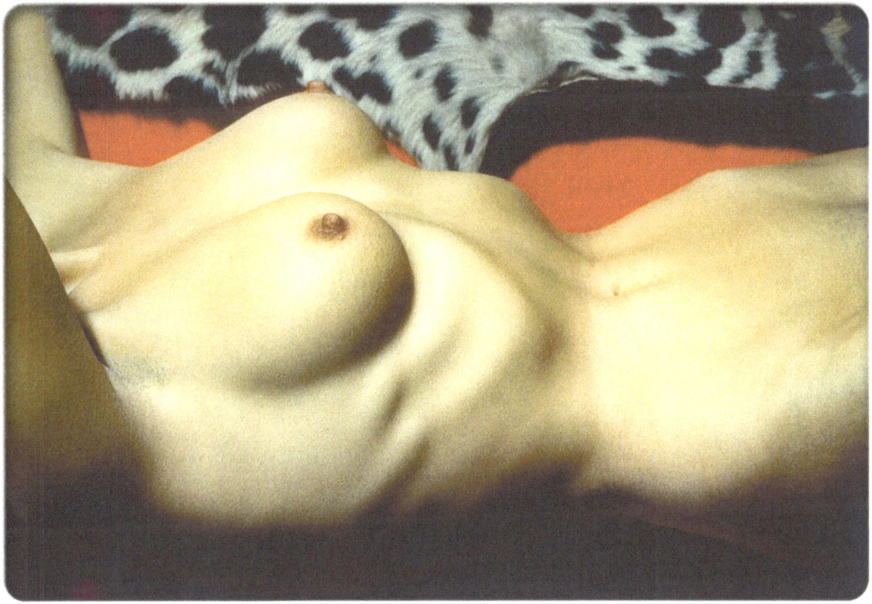

Colour Slide

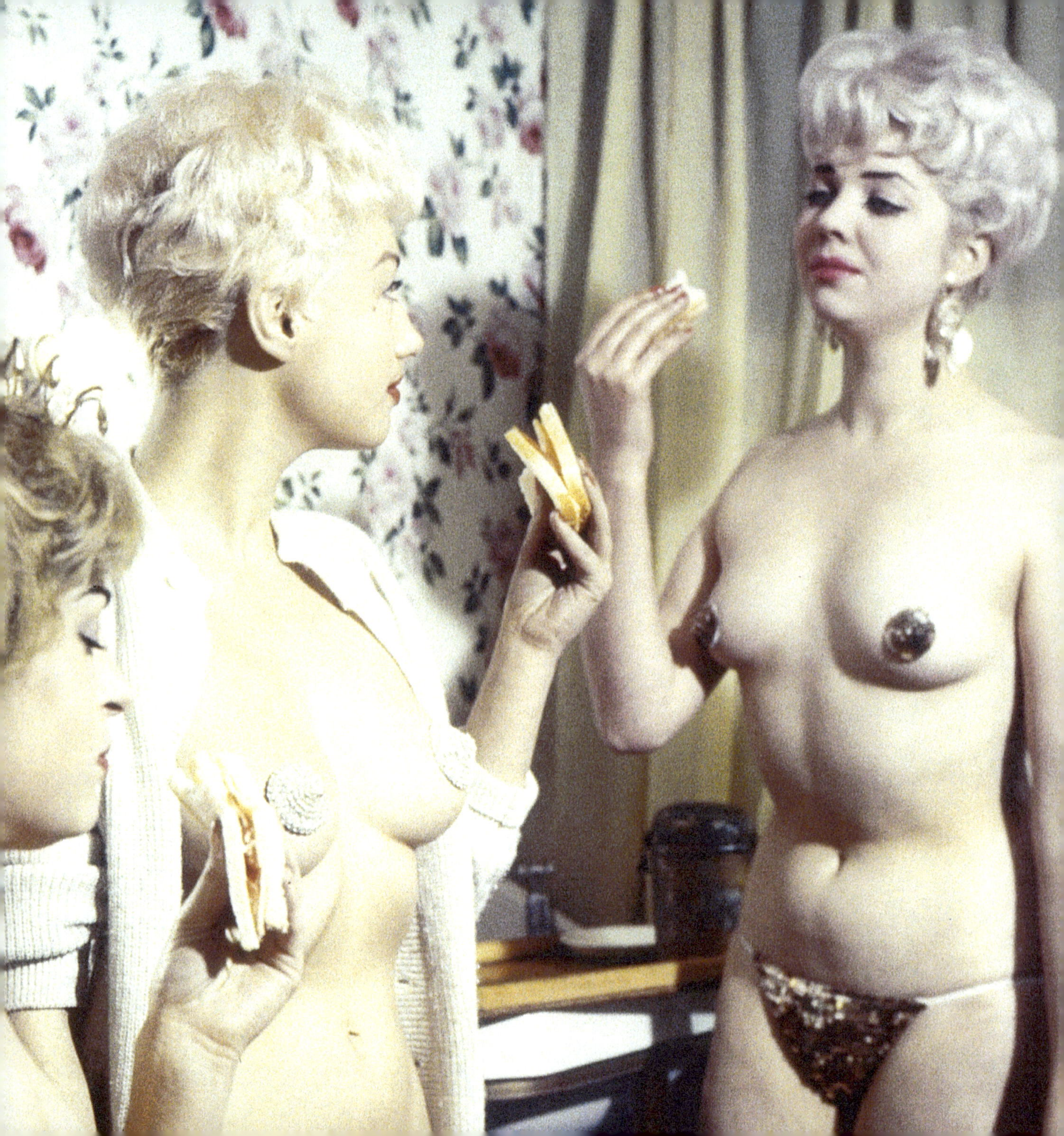

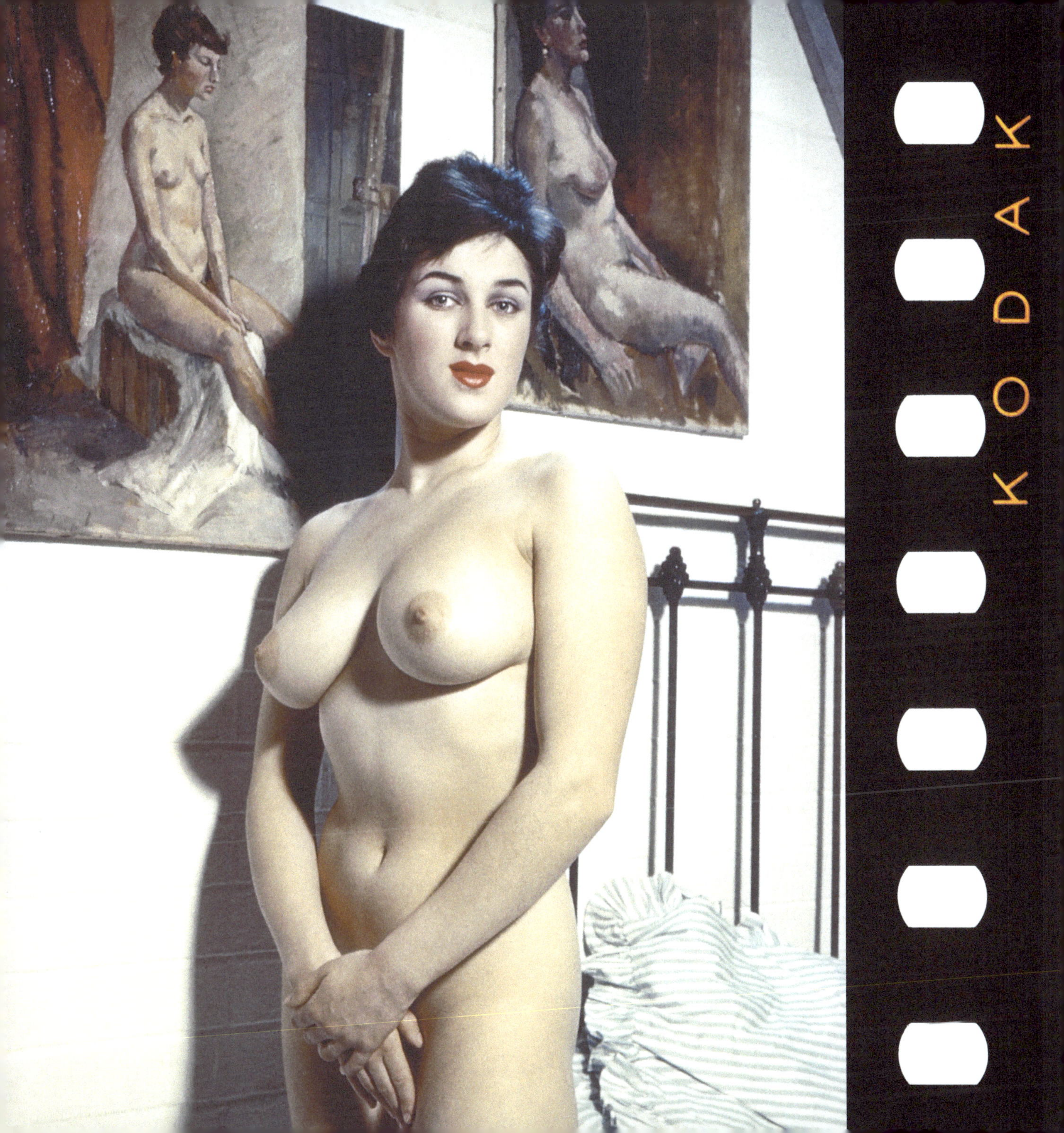
KODAK

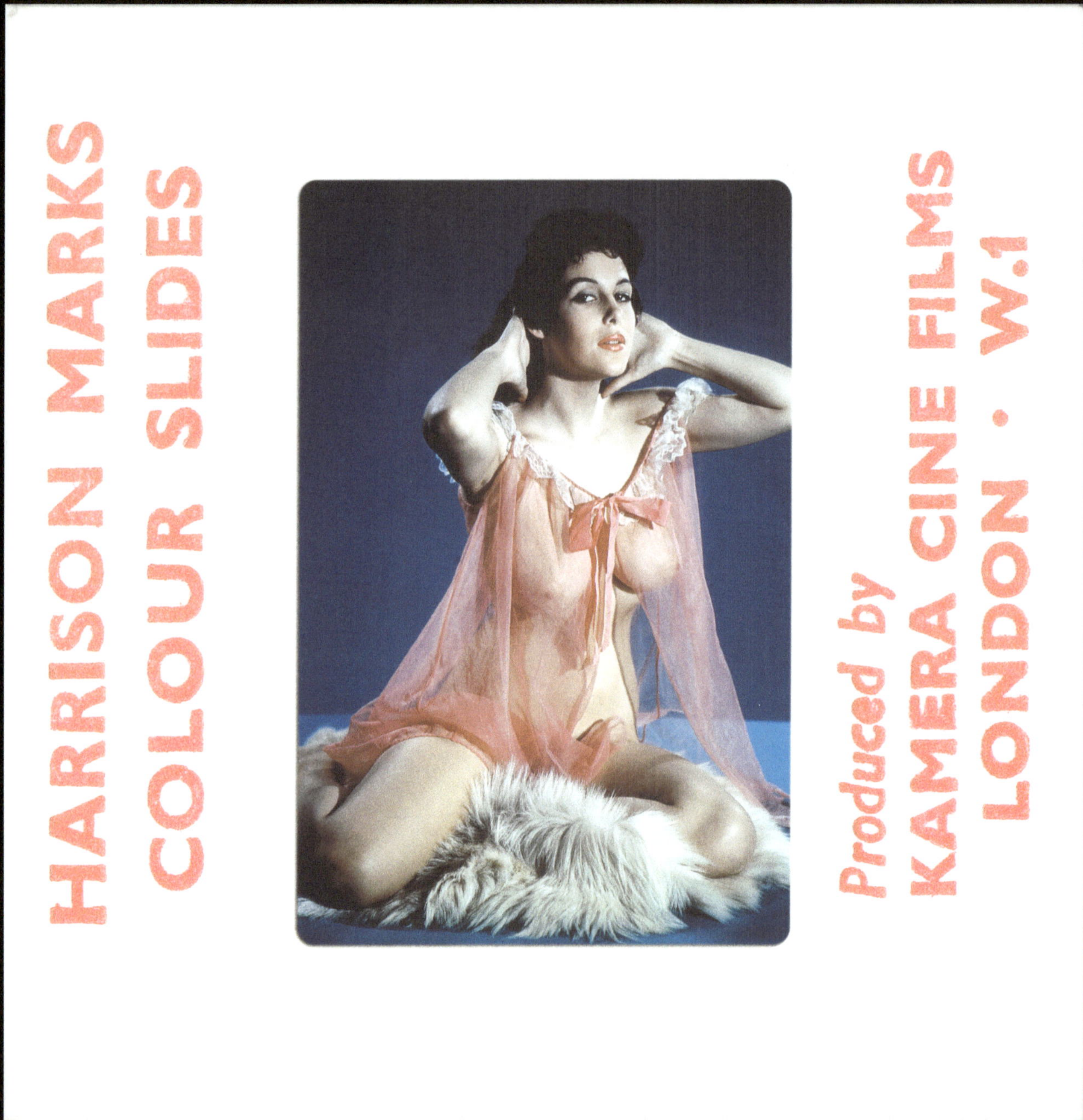
HARRISON MARKS
COLOUR SLIDES
Produced by
KAMERA CINE FILMS
LONDON · W.1

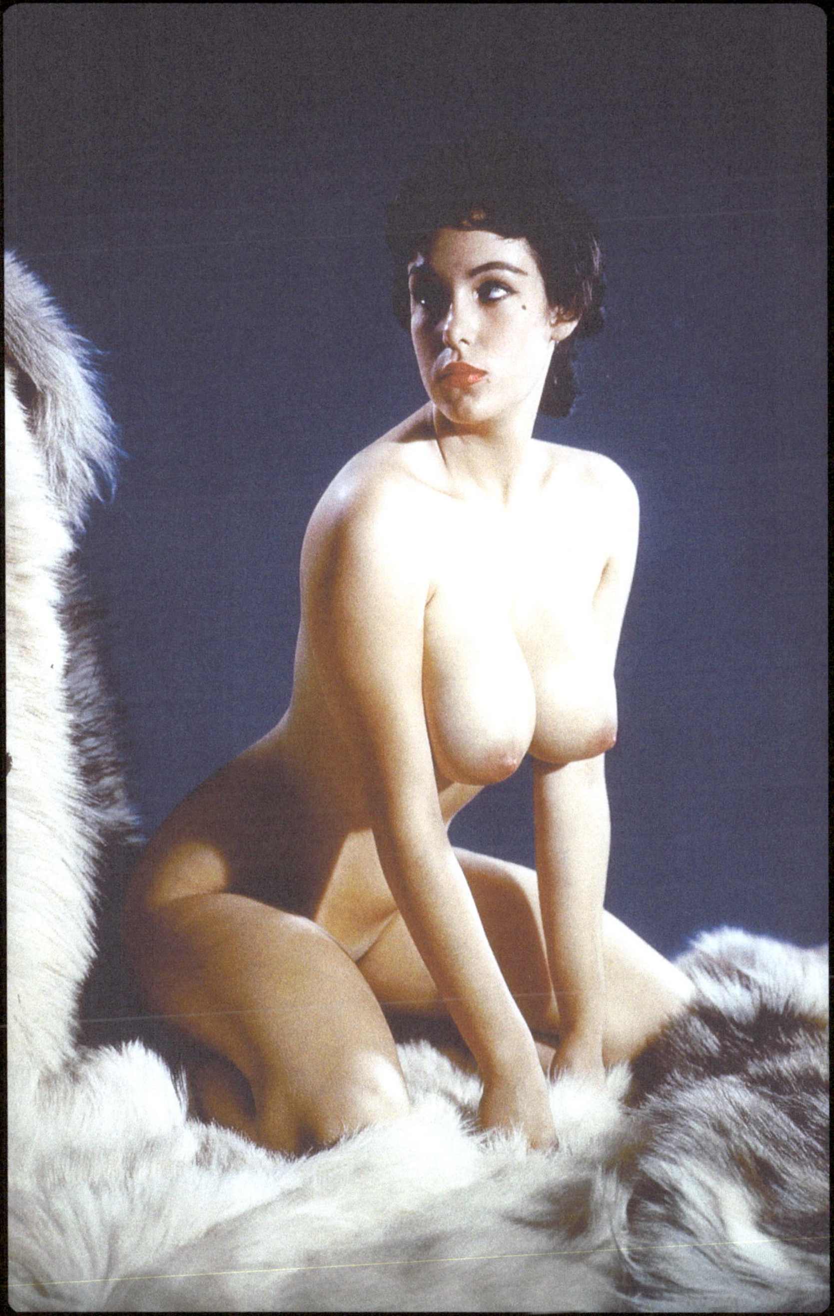

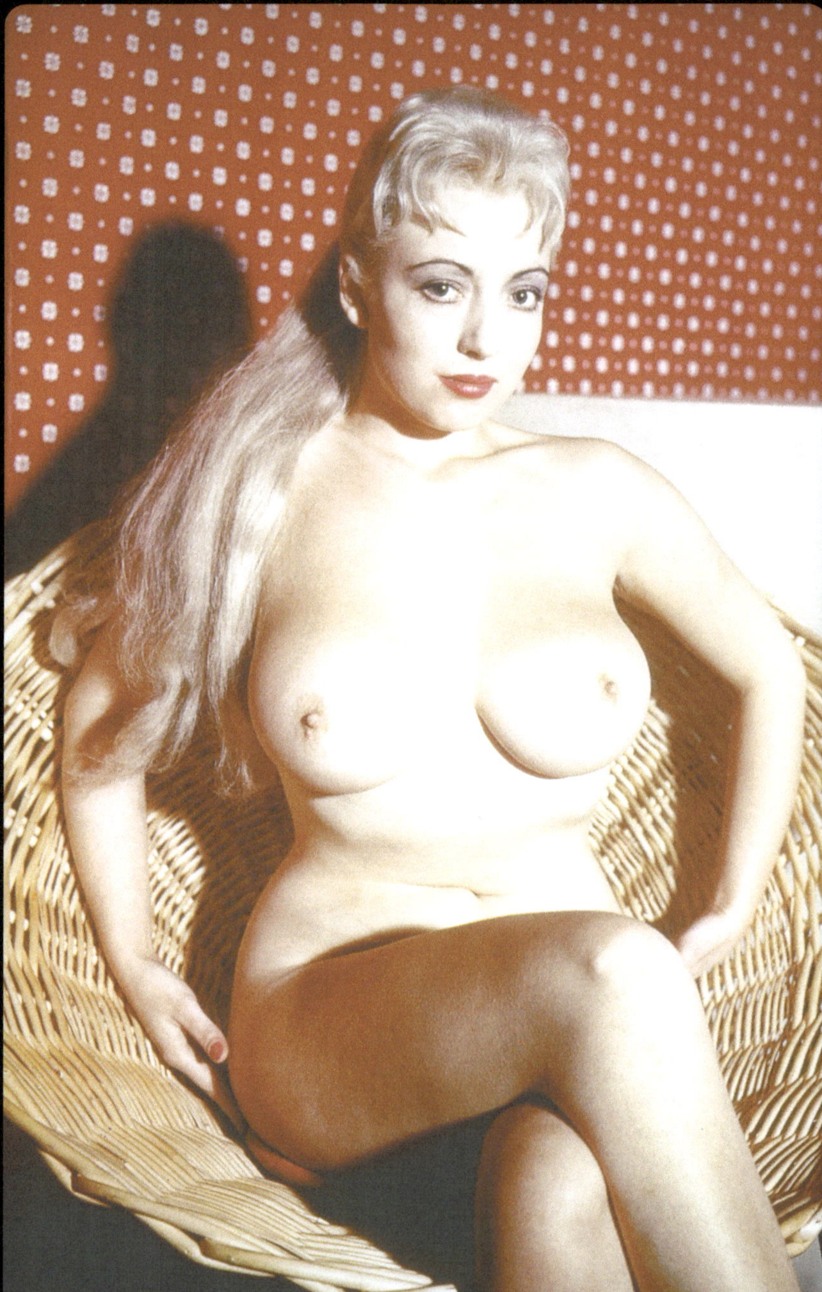

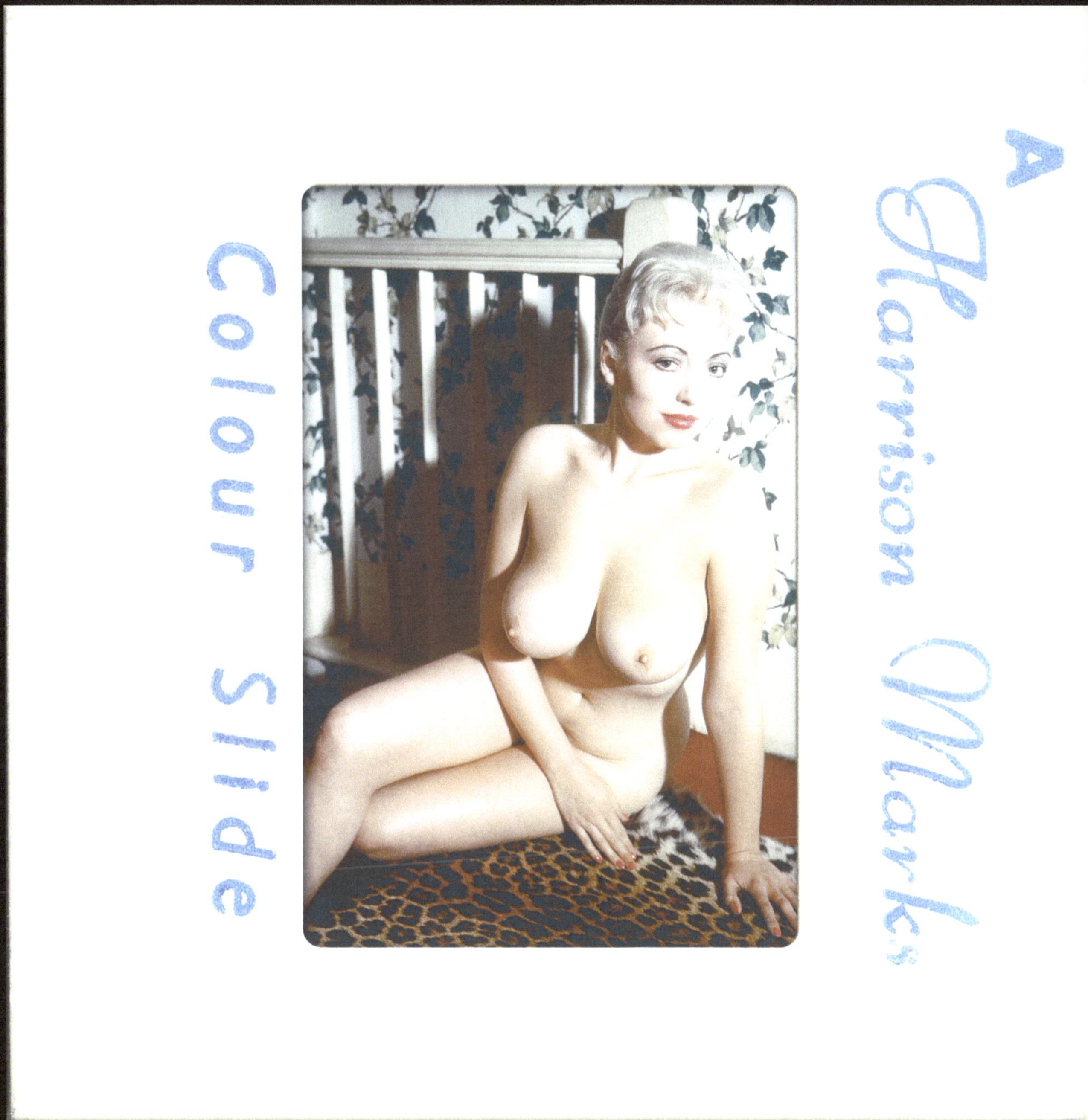
A Harrison Marks
Colour Slide

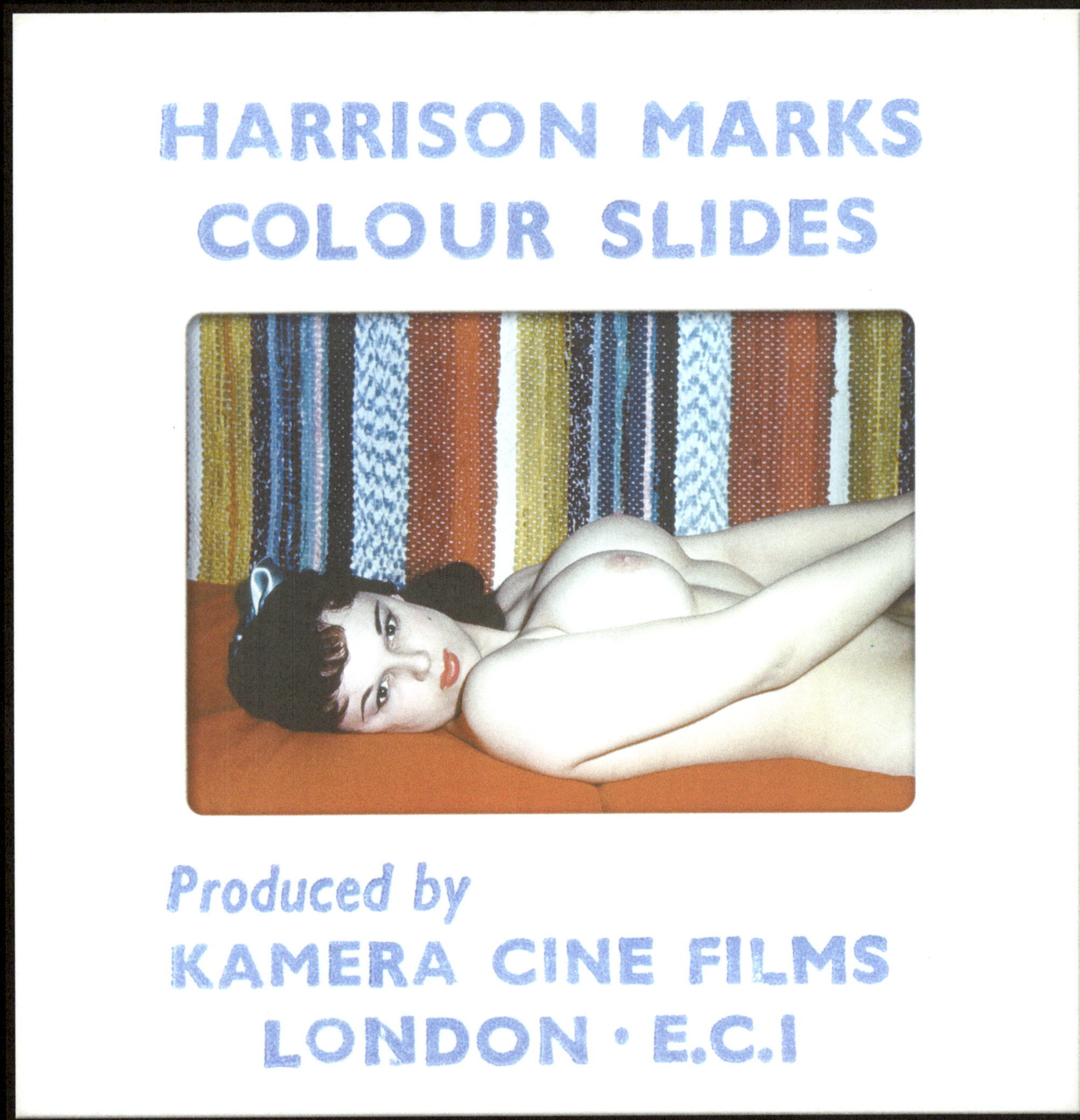
HARRISON MARKS
COLOUR SLIDES
Produced by
KAMERA CINE FILMS
LONDON · E.C.I

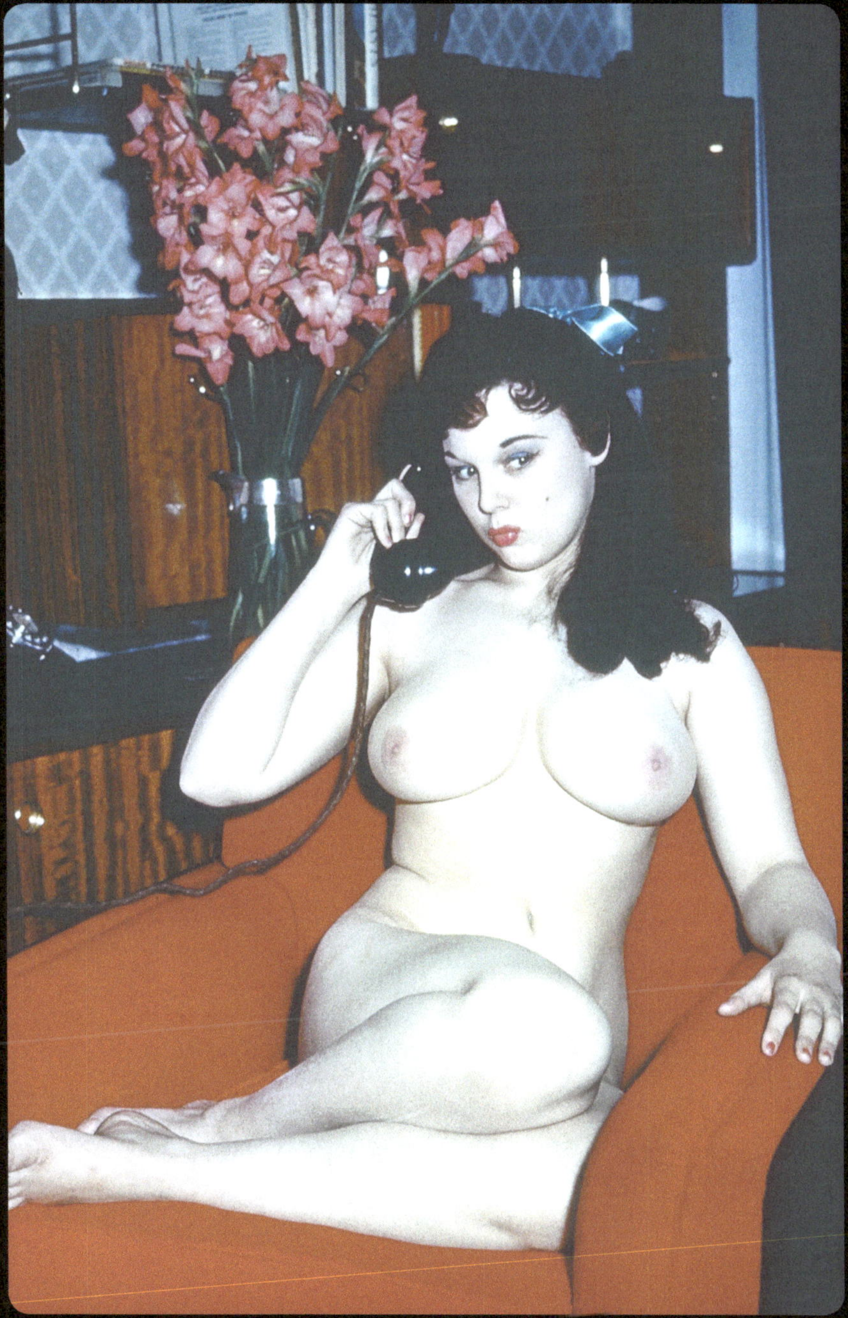

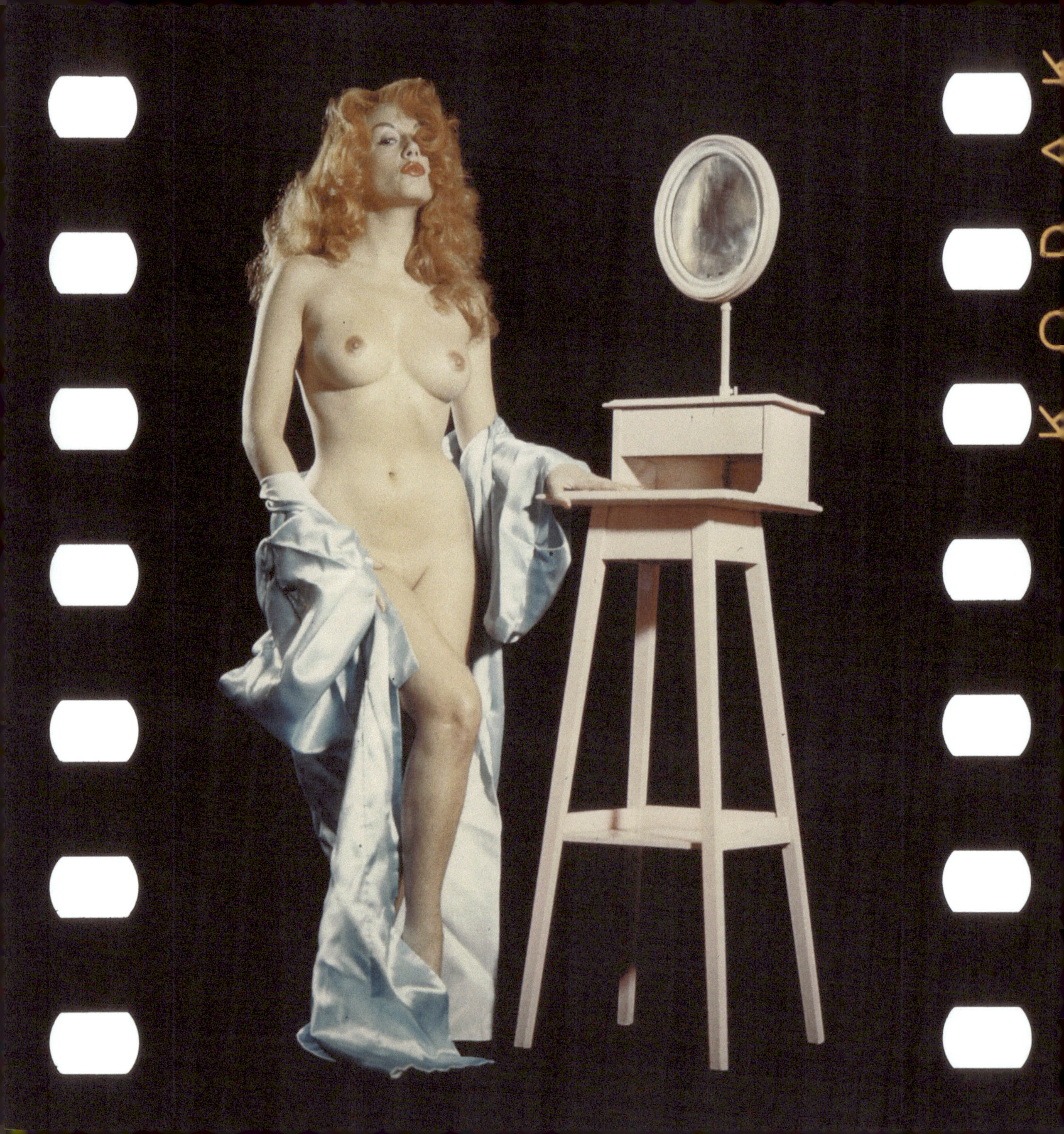
KODAK

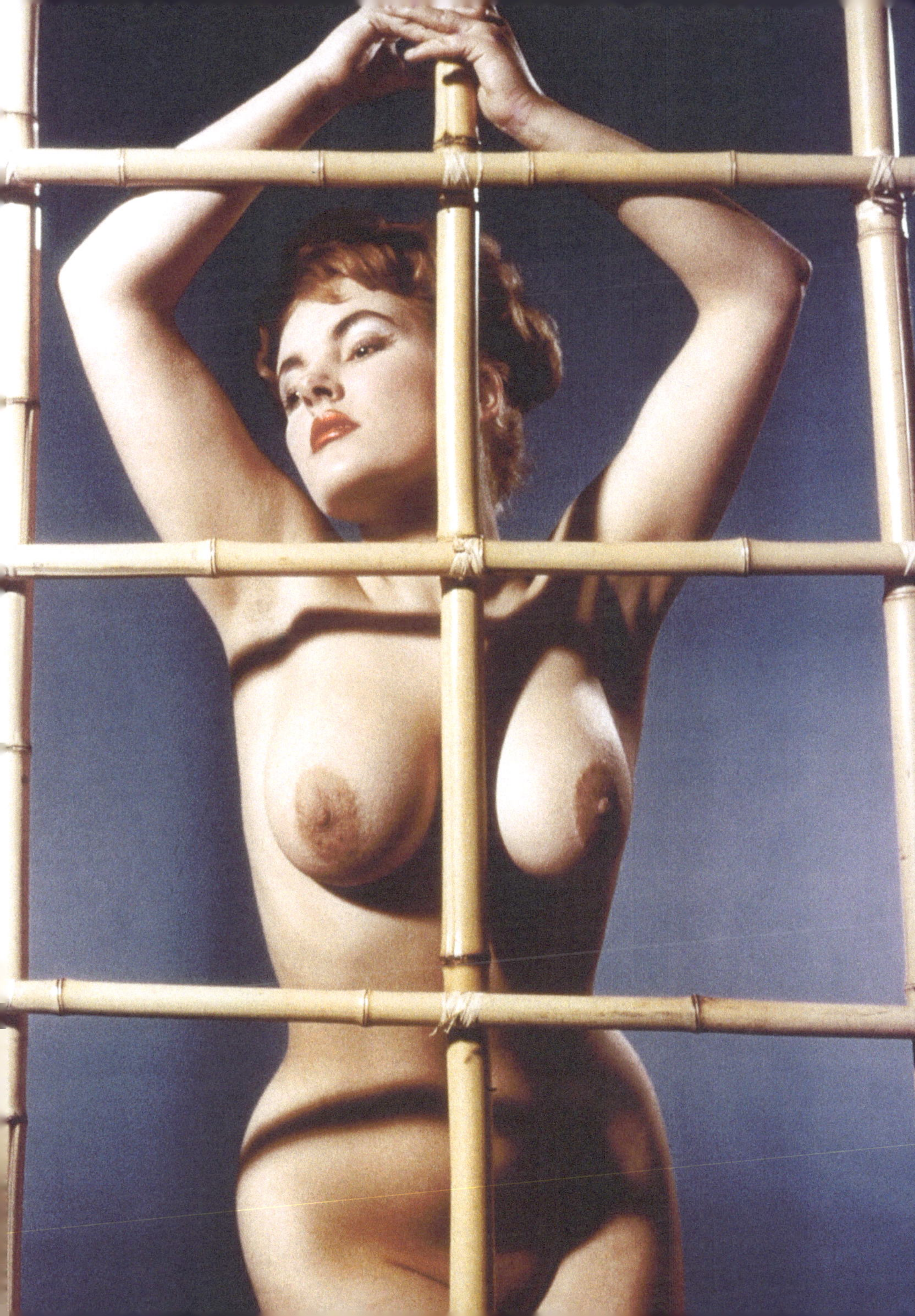

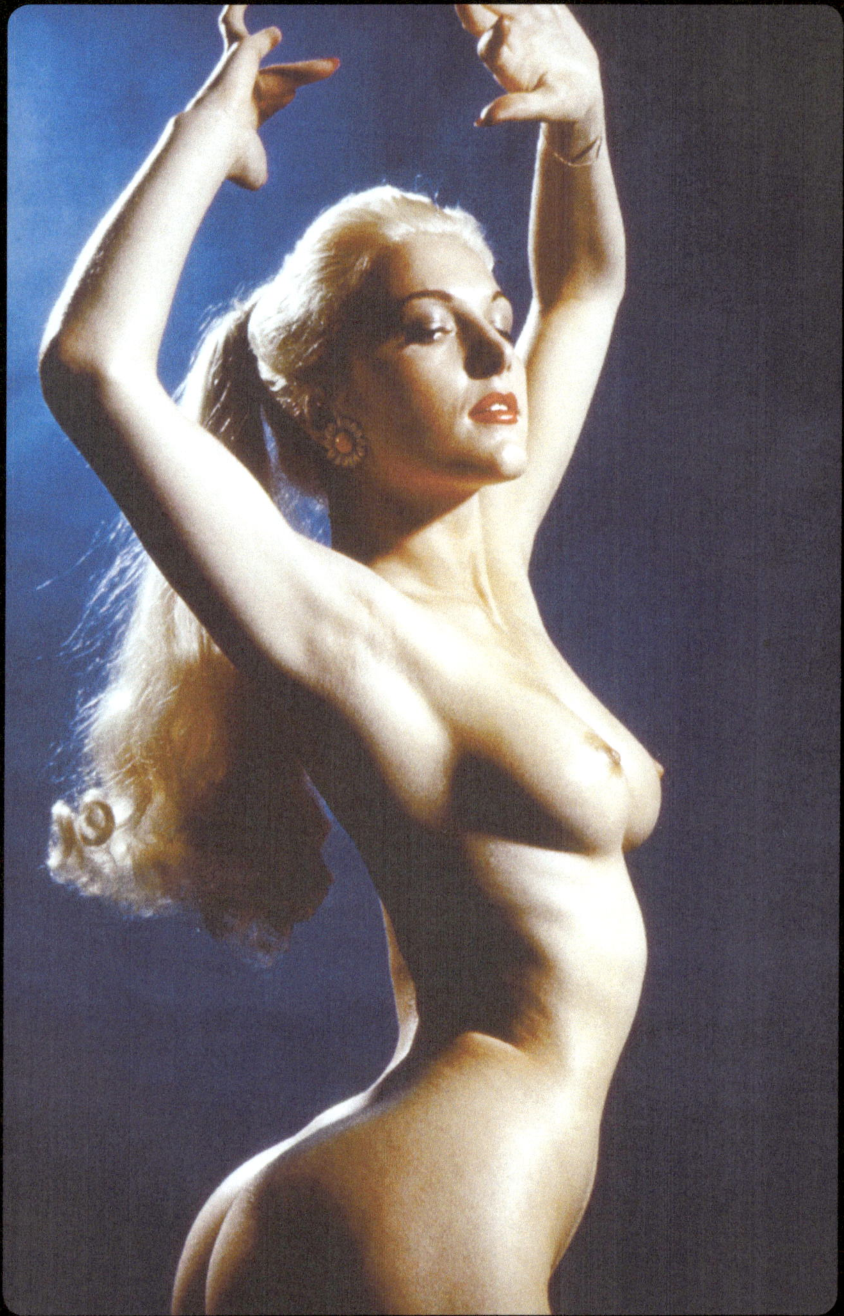

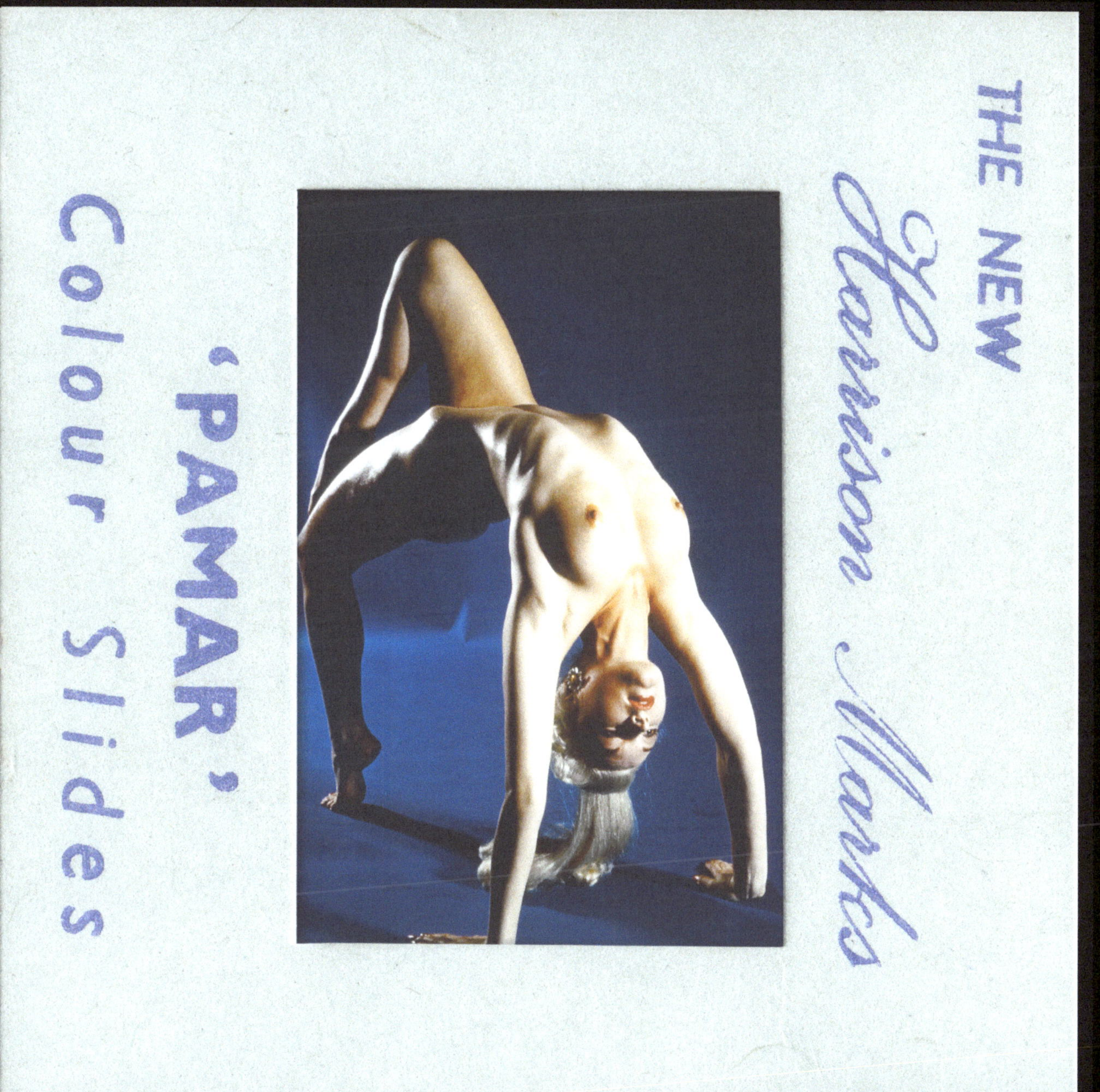
THE NEW
Harrison Marks
'PAMAR'
Colour Slides

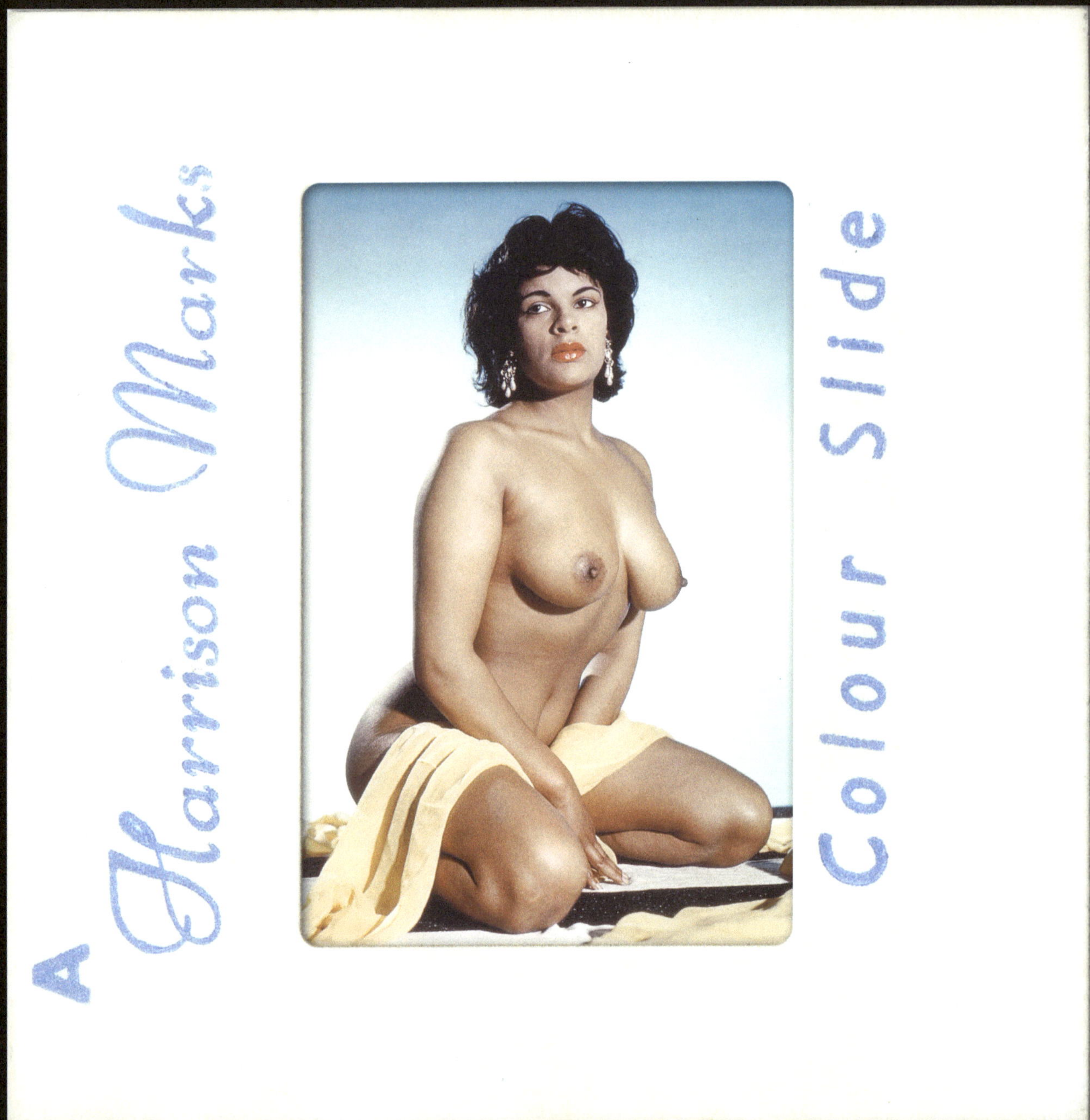
A Harrison Marks
Colour Slide

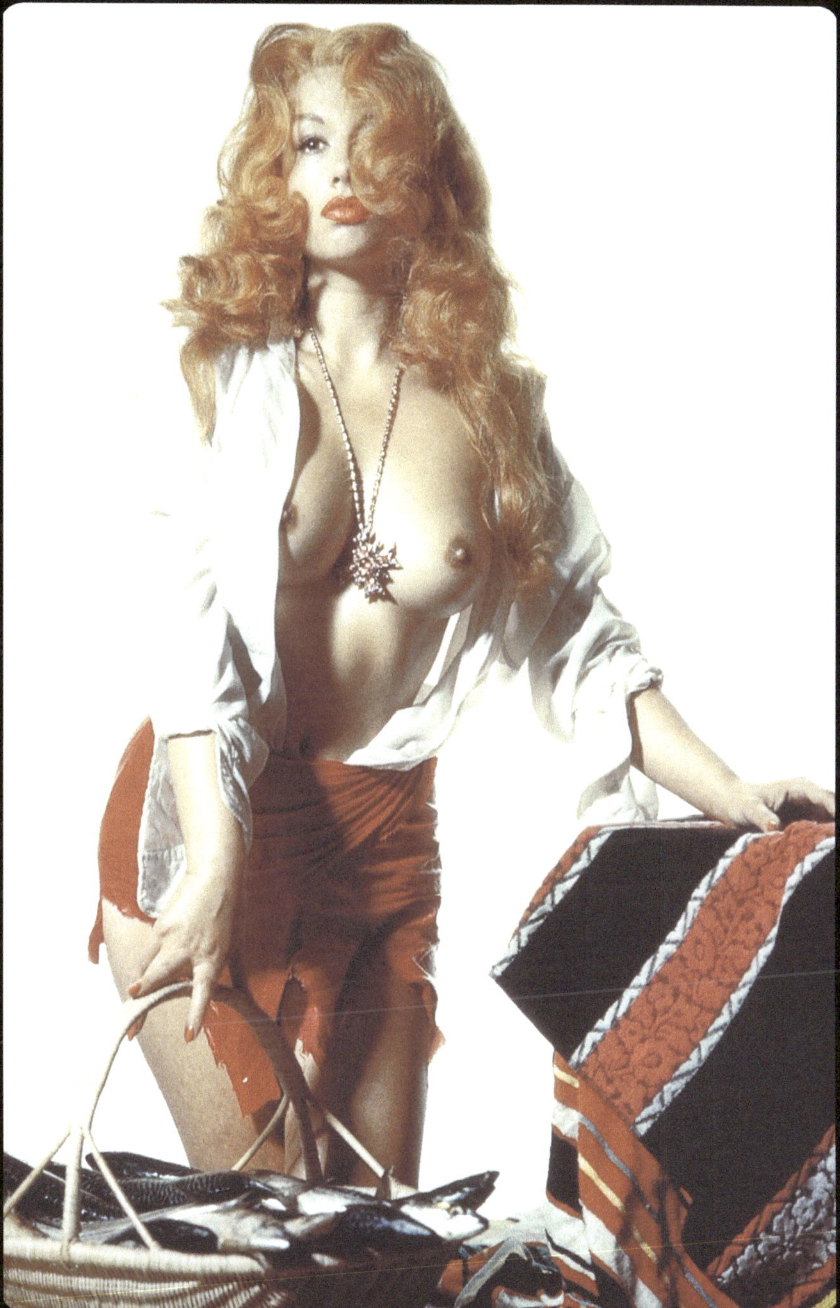

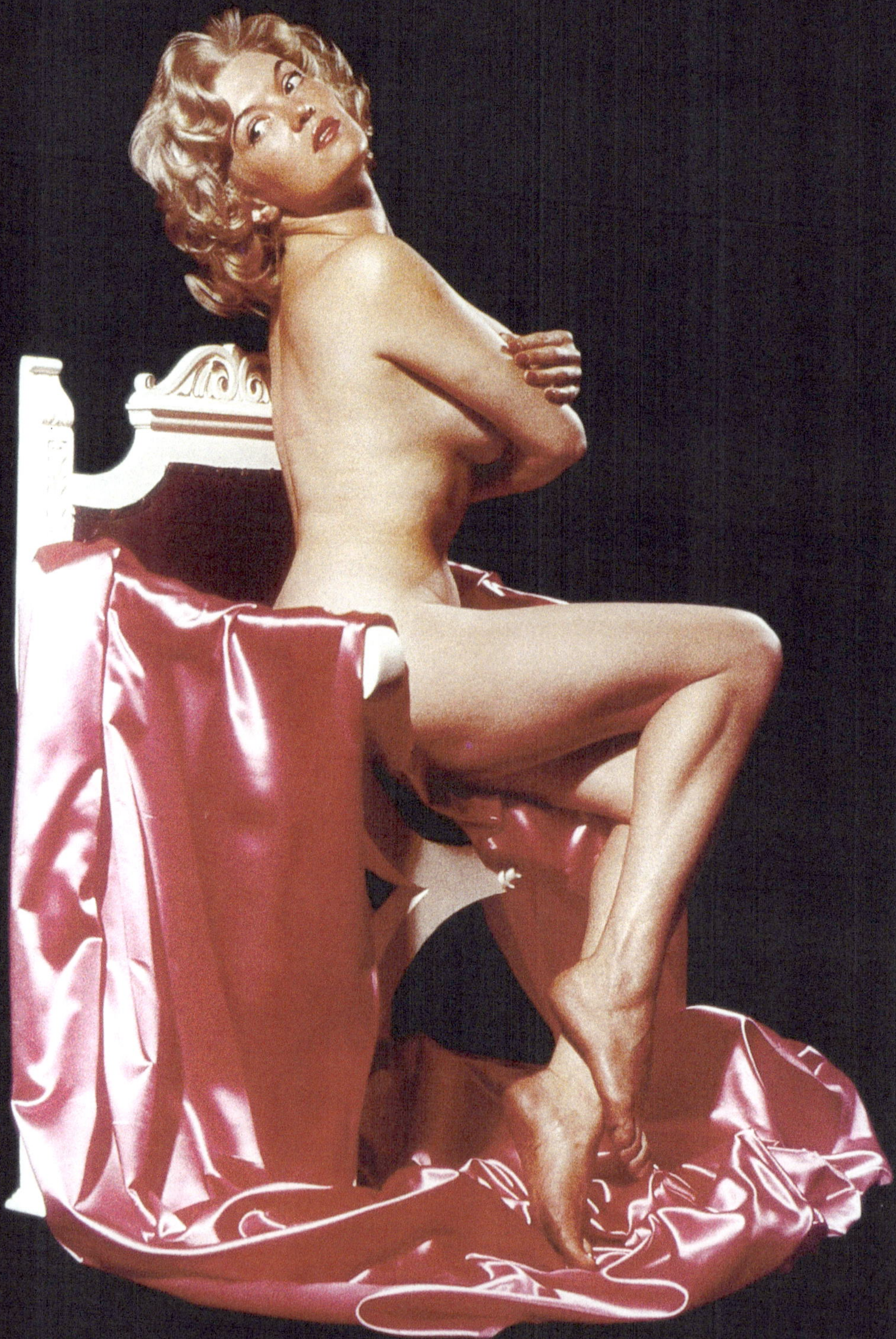

Model Index

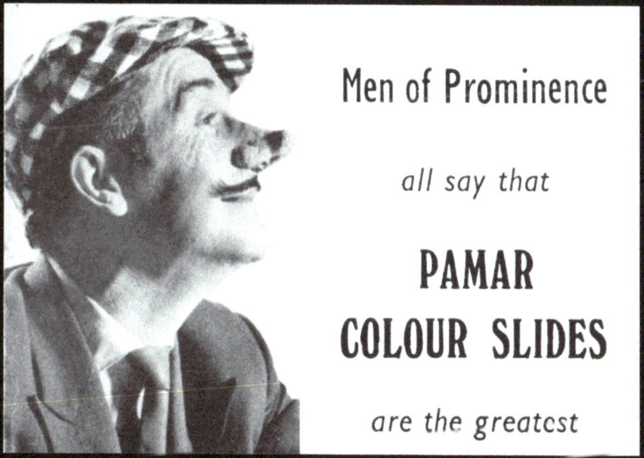

Men of Prominence
all say that
PAMAR
COLOUR SLIDES
are the greatest

WOLFBAIT

UNDER THE COUNTER CULTURE

Doing Rude Things
The history of the British sex film.

Cinema au Naturel
A history of nudist film.

Miniten: Rules of the Game
Invented in the 1930s, Miniten is a tennis-like game played by naturists.

Naked as Nature Intended
The epic tale of a nudist picture by Pamela Green, with photographs by Douglas "Dambuster" Webb, DFM.

The Naked Truth About Harrison Marks
The notorious biography by Franklyn Wood.

Past Masters of the Nude
An illustrated bibliography of nude photography books published in England from 1896 to 1960.

Amazons of Yesteryear
A rare, action-packed collection of images of wrestling women of the 1940s and 1950s.

Beauty Off-Duty
Relaxed, everyday moments caught on camera.

Naked in the Menagerie
A playful look at Eve accompanied by her animal friends.

Nudist Camp Follies – volumes 1 and 2
An intimate look at the natural and free atmosphere in Sun Clubs.

Nymphs and Naiads
Beauty unadorned and outdoors.

Poise and Pose
A magnificent series of photographs of female beauty taken in the studio.

Order online at wolfbait.co.uk

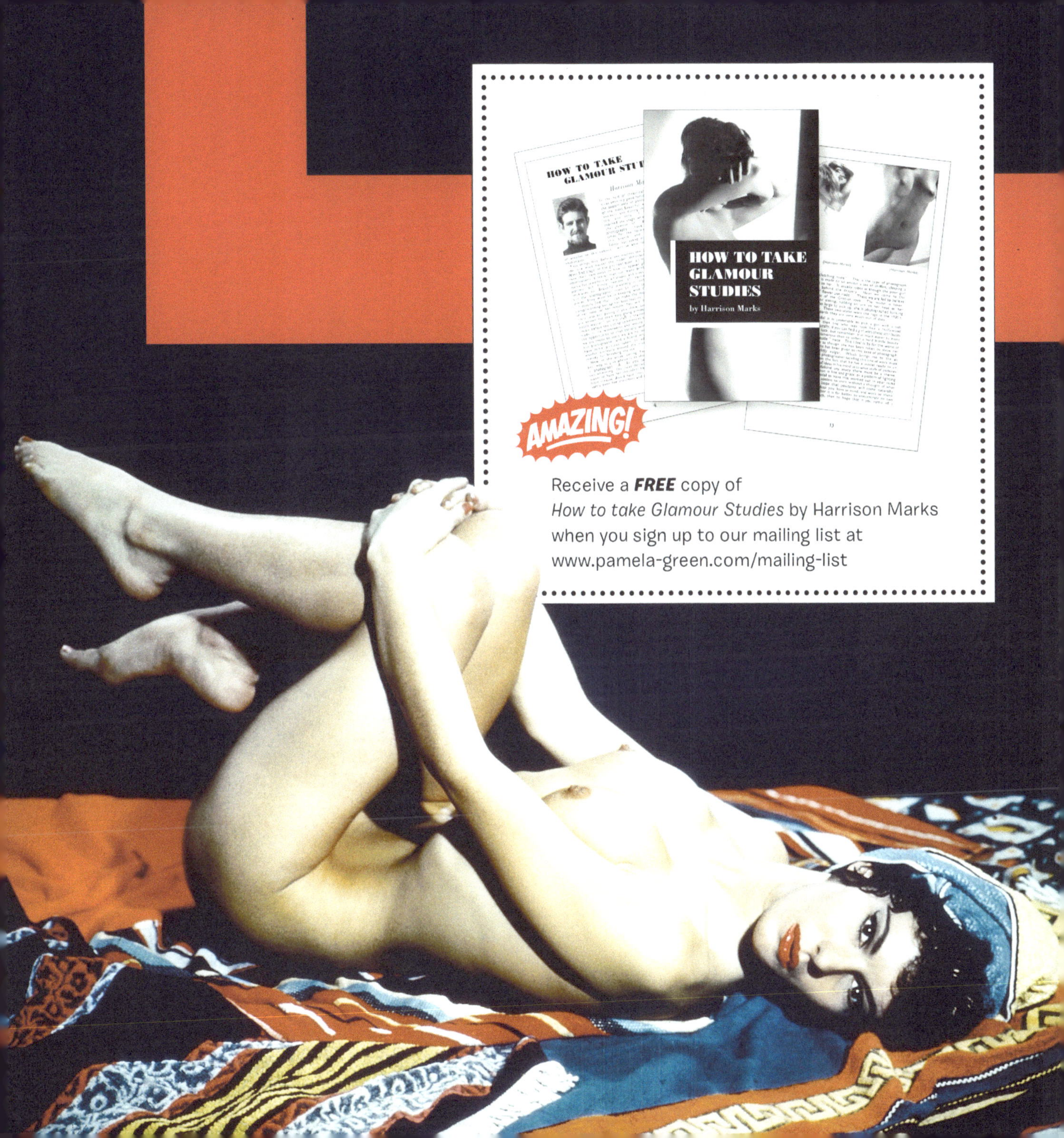
HOW TO TAKE
GLAMOUR STUDIES
by Harrison Marks
AMAZING!
Receive a ***FREE*** copy of
How to take Glamour Studies by Harrison Marks
when you sign up to our mailing list at
www.pamela-green.com/mailing-list

www.ingramcontent.com/pod-product-compliance
Ingram Content Group UK Ltd.
Pitfield, Milton Keynes, MK11 3LW, UK
UKHW061033310726
14089UKWH00010B/218

* 9 7 8 1 9 1 6 2 1 5 1 5 3 *